A STEP BY STEP GUIDE TO

CAKES

BISCUITS

& slices

A STEP BY STEP GUIDE TO

CAKES

BISCUITS

& slices

Colour
Library
Direct

When we test our recipes, we rate them for ease of preparation. The following cookery ratings appear on the recipes in this book.

Two symbols indicate the need for just a little more care and little more time.

A single Cooking with Confidence symbol indicates a recipe that is simple and generally quick to make – perfect for beginners.

Three symbols indicate special dishes that need more investment in time, care and patience – but the results are worth it.

CONTENTS

CAKES

BISCUITS & slices

Baking Basics

Making cakes is a pleasure – a rewarding form of relaxation.
Ensure worry-free success every time you bake by
following the information set out on these introductory pages.
That way, you can have your cake and eat it, too!

Measures and Equipment

A few essential pieces of equipment will streamline cake baking. It's well worth making the investment.

Measuring cups: For dry ingredients such as flour and sugar, it's important to have a set of four standard metric measuring cups – 1 cup, ½ cup, ⅓ cup and ¼ cup measures.

Place the cup measure on a flat surface (measuring will be inaccurate if you attempt to hold it) and spoon the dry ingredient lightly into it, levelling off with a flat-bladed knife. Don't shake or tap the cup.

Soft brown sugar is measured as a dry ingredient. Pack it down tightly in the specified measuring cup, to the point where it is level with the top. Use only dry measures for dry ingredients.

To measure liquid items such as milk and juice, use a standard metric measuring cup of heatproof plastic or glass with a pouring lip. The lines of measurement run down the cup's side. Place the cup on a board, add liquid to the required measure and check at eye level with the measurement marks.

Measuring spoons: Those used for cooking are different from flatware for serving and eating. They are essential for the accurate measuring of small amounts of dry and liquid ingredient. You need 1 tablespoon, 1 teaspooon, ½ teaspoon and ¼ teaspoon measures.

Kitchen scales: Useful for weighing butter. Conveniently, some blocks of butter have weight markings on the side of the wrapper; simply use a small, sharp knife to cut through the butter at the mark you require.

Scales are a help for measuring large quantities of dried and glacé fruits, nuts and chocolate. For those who prefer to measure by weight, not by volume, see the chart on page 112 for conversion of metric cup measures.

Metric or imperial? Do not attempt to combine metric and imperial measures. Use one system of measurement only, and stick with it.

Egg sizes: In all the recipes in this book, we have used eggs each with an average weight of 60 g.

Ovens: An accurate oven is possibly the most important piece of equipment for successful cake baking. Because ovens can lose their calibration, they should be checked every six months to ensure that correct temperatures and accurate readings are reached.

All ovens vary and not all oven thermometers are to be trusted. Be prepared to make slight adjustments to the temperatures and cooking times until you know your own oven well.

Always preheat the oven before you begin preparing your cake mixture.

For the best results when baking, position an oven rack in the lower third of the oven; this enables the top of the cake tin to be in approximately the middle of the oven. Centre the cake tin on the oven rack. If you are baking two cakes at the same time, stagger the tins so they are not placed directly beneath one another. If both are placed on the same rack, keep them away from the sides and back of the oven. They may need turning during the last third of the the cooking time to ensure an even result.

Electric beaters: An electric stand mixer is a vital piece of equipment; it

Place the dry ingredient in a measuring cup. Level it with a flat-bladed knife.

Pack soft brown sugar into measuring cup; press firmly with back of spoon.

To measure liquid, place jug on a flat surface. Measure liquid at eye level.

enables you to cream butter and sugar mixtures effortlessly to the correct consistency. It beats egg whites and egg white mixtures quickly and easily.

Adequate results can be obtained using a hand-held mixer or by mixing by hand if quantities are not too great. However, if you choose the latter, the mixing time increases considerably and care must be taken to achieve the correct consistency.

Food processors: These are ideal for blending ingredients together, but are unsuitable for creaming mixtures.

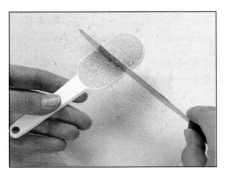

Place the dry ingredient in a measuring spoon. Level it with a flat-bladed knife.

Cake tins: Using the correct size of cake tin plays an important part in the success of the finished cake. There are many shapes and sizes of tin from which to choose. Aluminium ones give consistently good results. Avoid using shiny or very dark tins and glass bakeware. Listed are the tin sizes we used. Different manufacturers may produce slightly different sizes.

Changing tin sizes: If you wish to substitute one shape of tin for another, measure the volume of the batter and pour the same amount of water into the tin you intend to use. As long as the water does not come any higher than two thirds of the way up the tin, you can use it.

Useful extras: Two wire cake racks for cooling cakes; several wire sifters for flour and cocoa powder; a range of wooden and metal spoons; small to large glass mixing bowls; a small hand grater for rind; rubber and plastic spatulas; a long, serrated knife to level and slice cakes horizontally, and a flat-bladed or palette knife for smoothing on the icings and fillings.

Cake Tin Shapes and Sizes

1 **Ring Tin** 20 cm
2 **Deep Round Tin** 17/20/23 cm
3 **Shallow Round Tin** 17/20/23 cm
4 **Round Springform Tin** 20 cm
5 **Baba (Fluted) Tin** 20 cm
6 **Deep Fluted Ring Tin** 23 cm
7 **Loaf Tin** 21 x 14 x 7 cm
　Loaf Tin 23 x 13 x 7 cm
　Loaf Tin 25 x 15 x 5.5 cm
8 **Shallow Oblong Tin** 30 x 20 x 3 cm
　28 x 18 x 3 cm
9 **Long Bar Tin** 26 x 8 x 4.5 cm
10 **Shallow Patty Tin** 12 cup
11 **Deep Square Tin** 15/20/23 cm
12 **Shallow Swiss Roll Tin** 30 x 25 x 2 cm
13 **Oven Tray** 32 x 28 cm

Preparing Cake Tins

The way to prepare a cake tin varies according to the type of cake you are baking. Here are the general guidelines.

Butter cakes and chocolate cakes: They require tins that are greased and lined. You need to line the

To line square tins: Place tin base on a square of greaseproof paper; trace around it. Cut base out as marked. Cut a strip of greaseproof paper the same length as the circumference of the tin and about 1 cm deeper than the height.

Grease the base and sides of the tin with melted butter or oil, applying it with a pastry brush. Place the square of greaseproof paper on the base. Place the long strip of greaseproof around the sides of the tin, pressing it into the sides; grease base and sides of paper lining.

To line round tins: Place tin base on a square of greaseproof paper, trace around it. Cut base out as marked. Cut a strip of greaseproof paper the same length as the circumference of the tin and about 3 cm deeper than the height.

Fold down a cuff about 2 cm deep on one edge of the strip. Cut folded cuff diagonally at 2 cm intervals. Grease tin with melted butter or oil, applying it with a pastry brush.

Place strip in tin with folded side on base; press paper into base and side of the tin. Place the round of greasproof paper on base, grease base and side of paper lining.

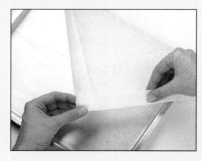

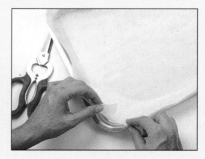

To line Swiss roll tins: Place tin base on a square of greaseproof paper; trace around it. Measure depth of tin, then measure paper from the marked line, and cut all around to 2 cm larger than the depth.

Crease paper along marked lines, cut paper to each corner. Grease tin with melted butter, applying it with a pastry brush. Press paper down into base and sides of tin; grease paper lining.

base and side/sides of the tins and grease the paper for these cakes. Fluted tins and baba tins are greased; if using anodised baba tins or if the cake mixture is very rich, you may need to lightly flour the baba tin, too.

Sponges: Tins must be greased, and their base lined and floured for easy removal of the cake.

Traditional fruit cakes and cakes rich with dried or glacé fruits: Tins need their base and side/sides lined with greaseproof paper; it is generally not necessary to grease the paper. A double thickness of brown paper is wrapped around the outside of the tin and secured with a paper clip before baking; this protects and insulates the cake during the long, slow baking time.

Greasing tins: Use melted, unsalted butter or oil. Apply evenly, smoothly and not too thickly, using a pastry brush. Vegetable baking sprays can be used to grease tins; apply in a well ventilated area away from heat sources.

Lining with paper: Greaseproof paper is the preferred paper for lining tins. Non-stick baking paper is also available and good results are achieved with this coated paper; it is not necessary to grease it.

Dusting: Let the greased tin or the greased paper dry off a little before dusting the tin with flour. Use plain flour, turning the tin to evenly coat the base and sides. Shake off the excess before spooning in the cake mixture. Some recipes call for the tin to dusted with desiccated coconut, finely ground breadcrumbs or nuts. Follow the same procedure as you would with flour.

Ingredients

Each ingredient used in cake baking has a specfic role.

Flour: This forms the structure of the cake. We have used plain flour and self-raising in our recipes. Plain flour (also known as all-purpose flour), has no raising agent. Self-raising flour is plain flour with baking powder added, that acts as the raising agent. To use plain flour in place of self-raising, add 2 standard metric teaspoons to each ¾ standard metric cup of plain flour. Sift flour and baking powder together three times before using.

Eggs: These are also essential to the structure of the cake. They bind the other ingredients together, and also add flavour and colour. We have used eggs each with an average weight of 60 g. For baking, eggs should be at room temperature. Take them out of the fridge an hour before required. Eggs separate far more easily when cold; separate white from yolk while cold; bring to room temperature before use.

Butter: Butter supplies flavour, texture and aroma. We used unsalted butter in all our recipes because it gives cakes a fuller, richer and sweeter flavour. Butter should be at room temperature (about 22°C) for it to cream correctly. If colder, it will not cream or aerate well. If it is too soft and oily, it will not aerate at all.

Margarine: This produces an adequate result; avoid low-fat margarine because it contains too much water.

Oil: In carrot and zucchini cakes, oil gives very moist results. Use a good quality vegetable oil; avoid olive oil or peanut oil; their flavours are too pronounced.

Sugar: It adds sweetness, colour, softness and fine grain to cakes. Fine-textured caster sugar is commonly used in baking. Granulated, all-purpose sugar is too difficult to cream and will only produce a coarse-textured cake. Icing sugar is too fine for general cake making. Soft brown sugar produces moist, flavoursome results in rich fruit cakes. Use soft dark brown sugar for a more intense flavour, if preferred.

Milk: The most commonly used liquid in cake baking. Others are yoghurt, buttermilk, sour cream and fruit juice.

Flavourings and essences: These should be of good quality. We used imitation vanilla essence in nearly all our recipes; it is widely available and inexpensive. Pure essences produce a delicious aroma and flavour. Their flavour is more intense – a little goes a long way.

Other flavourings such as finely grated orange or lemon rind, ground

Steps to Successful Cakes

- ☐ Read the recipe entirely beforehand. Assemble all the ingredients and equipment before proceeding.
- ☐ Preheat oven to correct temperature, prepare baking tins.
- ☐ Don't allow room temperature ingredients such as butter and eggs to get too warm.
- ☐ Measure ingredients accurately; do not judge quantities by eye but use standard metric measuring cups and spoons.
- ☐ Presift dry ingredients.
- ☐ Ensure correct creaming of butter and sugar mixtures; add eggs or egg yolks gradually.
- ☐ Don't overbeat egg whites.
- ☐ Take care with folding in procedures.
- ☐ Spoon or pour cake mixture into prepared cake tin, spread evenly into corners and smooth surface.
- ☐ Check oven temperature; avoid opening oven door until at least two thirds of the way through baking.
- ☐ Times given for cakes are approximate; the cooking time can vary according to the accuracy of the oven temperature and where the cake is placed.
- ☐ Stand cake in tin for specifed time before turning onto wire rack to cool.

spices, honey, treacle, cocoa or coffee powder and chocolate offer infinite variety to your baking. When grating orange or lemon rind, grate only the coloured surface of the skin, not the white, bitter pith.

Techniques

Sometimes a cake is described simply by its flavourings; for example, as a chocolate or coffee cake. Other times, cakes can be described by the nature of their presentation – teacakes or celebration cakes, for example.

Cakes are also classified by the method used to make them. In general, they'll fall into one of four categories: creaming; whisking (beating of whole eggs and/or egg whites); rubbing and quick mixing.

It is important to understand the differences between methods and to follow the correct procedures for each.

Creaming method: This is the most frequently used method in cake baking. It is used for light to rich butter cakes, teacakes, light fruit cakes, chocolate cakes and more. The proportion of butter to sugar varies from recipe to recipe.

Best results are obtained by beating butter (which is at room temperature) and sugar in a small glass mixing bowl with electric beaters until the mixture is light and creamy.

The mixture will almost double in volume and should have no trace of the sugar granules. Scrape the sides of the bowl with a spatula several times during the creaming process to make sure the sugar and butter are well incorporated. This intial creaming process can take up to seven or eight minutes. Whole eggs or egg yolks are then added. Be sure to beat these lightly before adding them to the butter mixture; add the beaten eggs gradually, beating thoroughly after each addition.

Essences, grated rind and other flavourings are added at this stage. The butter mixture is then transferred to a large mixing bowl. Use a large metal spoon to gently fold in the sifted dry ingredients and liquid alternately. Stir until just combined and the mixture is almost smooth.

Take care with this final stage, mixing the ingredients together lightly yet evenly; over-enthusiastic beating can undo previous good work and produce a heavy, coarse-textured cake.

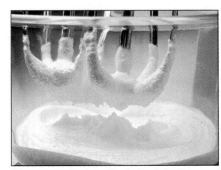

For creaming method, beat butter and sugar until light and creamy.

Whole eggs can be beaten with sugar over simmering water (Génoise-style).

Beat egg whites with electric beaters until stiff peaks form.

Gradually add the beaten egg yolks, continuing to use electric beaters.

Whisking method: This is generally used for sponges and light and airy Swiss rolls. Eggs are the chief ingredient, used whole or separated. Use the freshest eggs and have them at room temperature. Whole egg sponges are made by beating whole eggs in a small mixing bowl with electric beaters for 5 minutes or until thick and pale.

Sugar is added gradually, about a tablespoon at a time. Beat constantly until the sugar is dissolved and the mixture is pale yellow and glossy. The sifted dry ingredients are then quickly and lightly folded in.

Eggs can also be beaten whole with the sugar in a glass bowl over simmering water (Génoise style) until the mixture is very pale yellow and thick; a whisk or hand-held electric beaters can be used. The mixture is then removed from the heat and beaten with electric beaters until it has nearly doubled in volume. The sifted dry ingredients are then folded in.

Some recipes call for the eggs to be separated and beaten separately. Take care when separating eggs because just one small particle of egg yolk can ruin their beating quality. Separate one at a time into a small glass bowl; then transfer to the bowl for beating.

Beating the egg whites: Beating egg whites to the correct consistency is a vital stage in cake making. Use a glass bowl; make sure it is clean and dry. Use electric beaters to beat the egg whites until firm peaks form – the whites should hold a firm peak or curl when you lift the beaters out. Beating constantly, the sugar is then added gradually; beat until completely dissolved. The mixture should be very glossy and very thick; when you lift the beaters, the mixture should hold straight peaks.

The lightly beaten egg yolks are then added and the mixture is transferred to a large, glass mixing bowl. Use a metal spoon to fold in the sifted dry ingredients quickly and lightly.

The folding technique: This is also critical to success. It is the lightest way to combine two mixtures. Using a large metal spoon, fold in the dry ingredients, running the spoon along the underside of the bowl and up in one sweeping action – literally taking them under and over the egg mixture. Cut down through the centre of the bowl on the next fold, rotating the bowl as you fold. Repeat these actions until all of the ingredients are combined. Work quickly and lightly to ensure even dis-

tribution of ingredients and to avoid overmixing.

Rubbing method: Use for quick teacakes and economical fruit loaves.

The butter is chopped into small pieces and rubbed through the sifted dry ingredients until the mixture is a fine, crumbly texture. Use only your fingertips, lifting the flour from the bowl as you rub to evenly distribute the butter.

Liquid ingredients are combined and stirred into the flour mixture with a flat-bladed knife until the mixture comes together. Generally, cakes made by this method are best eaten the day they are made.

Quick mix method: This fast and simple method is gaining popularity. Use for cakes such as carrot and zucchini or easy chocolate cakes.

Vegetable oil or butter is used; the butter is melted with flavourings such as brown sugar or chocolate and then poured over the sifted dry ingredients. Make a well in the centre of the dry ingredients beforehand. Stir mixture with a wooden spoon or whisk until ingredients are evenly combined. The beaten eggs are then stirred in; care must be taken not to overmix.

Decorating Your Cake

Before you can ice or fill your cake, you will need to prepare it. Handle your cake with care at this stage.

Slicing Cakes

Always work with completely cooled cakes when decorating, unless the recipe states otherwise. If the cake is even slightly warm, it will be difficult to handle and there is every possibility that it will crack or break when sliced.

Some cakes dome slightly when baked and may need trimming before

Fold in flour with metal spoon; run it along bowl base in one sweeping action.

Quick mix method: Melted butter and sugar are poured on dry ingredients.

Testing if a cake is cooked: A cake is cooked when it begins to shrink from the sides of the tin and is lightly golden on top. If pressed with a finger, it should spring back into shape at once. The exception would be a very rich cake such as a fruit one which may retain a slight impression and yet still be cooked.

As a final check, insert a fine skewer in the centre; it should come out clean, without any moisture.

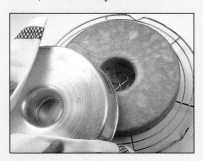

Cooling the cake: A cake is quite fragile when removed from the oven. It is best to leave it in its tin for the specifed time before turning it onto a wire rack to cool. Leave the cake on the wire rack until completely cold.

If a cake seems to be stuck to the tin, gently run a flat-bladed knife around the sides to release it. Cakes lined with paper are easiest to release; as you turn out the cake, use the paper to gently ease its passage. Remove the paper lining immediately. Wire cake racks can be sprayed with vegetable baking spray occasionally to prevent the warm cake sticking to them.

Brush loose crumbs off the cake with a pastry brush for a smooth finish.

Storage: As a general guide, you can store most cakes for up to three days in an airtight container. Fillings and icings make cakes more perishable.

Fruit cakes can be stored in the refrigerator for up to two months, covered with several layers of plastic wrap. See each of our recipes for specific storage guidelines for each cake.

Cakes can be successfully frozen. Best results are obtained when they are frozen uniced and unfilled. Open-freeze cakes to preserve shape. To do this, place on a tray in the freezer without covering. When frozen, wrap in plastic wrap and aluminium foil, excluding as much air as possible. Place in a rigid container for added protection. Label and date the cake. Store for up to three months or to the specified time. To defrost, loosen wrapping and leave at room temperature until thawed.

Using a flat-bladed knife, spread filling to within 5 mm of the cake edge.

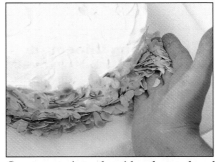

icing to give a better appearance. Use a long, sharp, serrated knife to slice off the dome. Cut only enough cake to give an even surface. Cut with a gentle sawing motion, using your other hand to steady the cake while you slice. Turn the cake over onto the serving plate, base side up, before icing.

Many cakes are cut in half or in one or more layers horizontally before they are filled. To make the job easy, mark the midpoint round the side of the cake with toothpicks. Use a long, sharp, serrated knife for slicing the cake; use a gentle sawing action. Repeat marking and cutting procedure for each layer.

Scoop nuts into the side of your hand and gently press them onto side of cake.

Icing and Filling Cakes

To achieve a good finish when icing, turn the cake over so the base side is up. Use a pastry brush to brush off any loose crumbs. Spread icing over the cake using a flat-bladed knife. The result will be a smooth iced surface.

To assemble layered cakes, slice horizontally as described. Place a dab of icing or filling on a serving plate. Place the first cake layer on top (the icing will stop it moving), centring it on the plate. Brush with jam or liquid, then spread evenly with the specified amount of filling mixture. Using a flat-bladed knife or metal spatula, spread the filling to within about 5 mm of the edge of the cake.

Slice off dome. Cut with gentle, sawing motion. Use other hand to steady cake.

Mark midpoint around cake with toothpicks; slice with sharp, serrated knife.

Using a vegetable peeler, shave curls of chocolate from flat side of block.

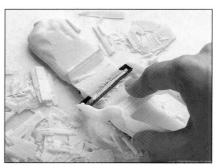

Pour melted chocolate onto a marble board; let set. Shave off chocolate.

Piping Bags

Here is quick and easy way to make a small, paper piping bag. This is an ideal 'tool' to use when working with fine icing and when icing a cake with melted chocolate.

Cut a 25 cm square of strong greaseproof paper and fold it in half diagonally to form a triangle. Working with the long side at the bottom, roll a corner to the centre and tape in place. Wrap the other corner around to the back and tape it in place. Use scissors to snip off the tip of the bag to suit the size of decorating you will be doing. You can also drop a small nozzle into the bag for icing.

Using a knife or metal spatula, half-fill the bag with melted chocolate or icing. Fold in the top, then roll the top down to the level of the icing to seal the bag. With your writing hand, grip the bag at the top with the full end resting in your palm. Use pressure from the palm of your hand to push the icing through the hole. Practice will show how to vary the pressure and achieve a good flow of icing.

Decorating Ideas

Chocolate Decorations, Shavings: Decorate the cake with chocolate shavings, simply by using a vegetable peeler to shave off curls from the flat side of a block of chocolate. Use long, even strokes. Work over greaseproof paper or a plate. For best results, the chocolate should be warmed, but only sufficiently to enable you to work it; it must not be melting. Leave chocolate in a warm spot for 10 to 15 minutes before shaving. Spoon or shake the shavings onto the iced cake.

Another version of curls is made by pouring 100 g melted chocolate onto a marble or Laminex board in a 4 cm wide strip. Smooth the surface, allow

Melting Chocolate

Some of the decorating ideas in this book require using melted chocolate. Care must be taken when melting chocolate in order to achieve good results.

Chop the chocolate into even-sized pieces and place in a glass bowl. Place bowl over a pan of simmering water; stir gently until chocolate has melted. Do not allow a drop of water to fall on the chocolate or it will immediately stiffen dramatically and be unworkable for decoration purposes. Cool chocolate slightly before use.

Place strips of greaseproof paper in a pattern. Dust with sifted icing sugar.

Place the second layer on top and spread with the filling mixture, in the same way as described above. Place the final layer, base side up, on the top. Spread a thin layer of cream or of frosting around the sides and top of the cake to seal in any crumbs and to fill any gaps. Dip the knife or spatula into hot water as you spread to make it a little easier to work. Wipe the knife with a clean cloth before you continue.

Spread a final layer of cream or frosting evenly around the sides and

then the top of the cake, blending at the edges. Use even strokes.

The edges of the cake can be decorated very effectively with toasted nuts. This is easier than it sounds. Simply press the nuts into the side of the cake using your hand. Scoop them up and push them gently into the cream or frosting, continuing around the cake until it is evenly covered. To finish, use a pastry brush to sweep away any loose nuts that have fallen on the serving plate.

Feather cake by drawing the point of a skewer from centre circle to outer edge.

Mark semi-set chocolate into wedges. Refrigerate. Peel away foil.

Mark semi-set chocolate into squares. Refrigerate. Peel away foil.

chocolate to set. Shave off strips with a vegetable peeler, using long strokes.

Sifted icing sugar: Cut strips of greaseproof paper about 1 cm wide, place in a pattern on top of the cake. Dust with sifted icing sugar. Carefully lift paper off, leaving a clear pattern. Use pretty paper doileys to achieve the same look.

Feathering: Ice the cake with dark icing and use light icing or melted chocolate to create a striking marbled effect. Place the melted chocolate or light icing in a paper piping bag and pipe concentric circles onto the icing. Draw the point on a knife or skewer from the the centre circle to the outside edge. Clean skewer and repeat, working around cake in wedges to produce a feathering effect.

Wedges: Cover the base of a 20 cm round tin with foil. Spread about 150 g melted chocolate evenly over it and refrigerate until semi-set. Using a sharp, flat-bladed knife, carefully mark the chocolate into 12 even wedges. Return to refrigerator until chocolate is completely set. Peel away foil.

Squares: These are an easy and impressive way to decorate the sides of a cake. Cover the base of a 32 x 28 cm oven tray with foil. Spread 200 g

melted chocolate evenly over it, swirl a fork lightly through the chocolate to create a wavy effect. Make sure you don't push it to the base. Refrigerate until semi-set. Using a sharp, flat-bladed knife and a ruler, mark chocolate into 6 cm squares. Return tray to refrigerator until chocolate is completely set. Peel away foil. Carefully press chocolate squares around the edges of the iced cake.

Lattice circles and silhouettes: Mark a sheet of baking paper with small circles, using a 3 cm cutter as a guide. Alternatively, mark squares, rectangles or triangles with a pencil. Melt about 150 g chocolate and place in a paper piping bag.

Applying a light pressure, pipe an outline of chocolate around the shape and fill it in with squiggly lines. Other shapes can also be most effective; try stars or flowers. Refrigerate until set. Use a flat-bladed knife to remove the decorations carefully from the baking paper, and place them on cake.

Cut-outs: The kids can make these! Cover the base of a shallow, 30 x 20 cm oblong tin with foil. Spread 250 g melted chocolate evenly over the base. Refrigerate until semi-set. Use small, sharp cutters to mark different shapes.

Use rounds and fluted rounds or other fancy shapes. Use to decorate the sides or the top of the iced cake.

Chocolate curls: These take a little time, practice and patience to master. Spread 250 g melted chocolate onto a marble or Laminex board to a depth of 1 cm, smoothing the surface lightly. Allow to cool until almost set. Use a sharp, flat-bladed knife; hold it horizontally. Applying constant pressure to the blade with both hands, pull the knife towards you. Varying the pressure on the blade will determine how thick or thin the curls will be.

Shapes: Boxes of very thin squares of chocolate are produced by several confectionery companies and are ideal, ready-made decorations.

Nuts and sprinkles: Sprinkle the top of a simple iced cake with finely chopped, toasted nuts, with coconut or with chocolate or coloured sprinkles. Decorate the outer edge of the iced cake with whole nuts or glacé cherries.

Marzipan fruits: When time is at a premium and you need a quick and easy, ready-made decoration, you can purchase a range of marzipan fruits from confectioners and also some good cake shops. These are most attractive, colourful and professional-looking.

Lattice shapes: Mark various shapes on greaseproof; pipe outlines of chocolate.

Chocolate cut-outs: Press a variety of sharp cutters into semi-set chocolate.

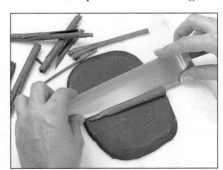

Chocolate curls: Hold knife horizontally. Apply constant pressure to blade.

SPONGE CAKES

CLASSIC SPONGE

Preparation time: 30 minutes
Cooking time: 20 minutes
Makes one 20 cm round layer cake

1 cup self-raising flour
4 eggs, separated
2/3 cup caster sugar
2/3 cup cream
1 teaspoon imitation vanilla
    essence
1/2 cup strawberry jam
icing sugar, for decoration

➤ PREHEAT OVEN to moderate 180°C. Brush two shallow, 20 cm round sandwich tins with melted butter or oil. Line bases with paper. Dust tins lightly with flour, shake off excess.

1 Sift the flour three times onto greaseproof paper.
Place egg whites in small, clean, dry mixing bowl. Using electric beaters, beat until firm peaks form. Add sugar gradually, beating constantly until it has dissolved and mixture is glossy and thick.

2 Add the beaten egg yolks, beat for a further 20 seconds. Transfer mixture to large mixing bowl. Using a metal spoon, fold in flour quickly and lightly.

3 Spread the mixture evenly into prepared tins. Bake for 20 minutes or until sponges are lightly golden and shrink from sides of tins. Leave the sponges in tins for 5 minutes before turning onto wire rack to cool.
Using electric beaters, beat cream and essence in small bowl until stiff peaks form. Spread jam on both sponges. Spread cream on one sponge layer using a flat-bladed knife. Top with other layer. Dust with sifted icing sugar just before serving.

COOK'S FILE

Storage time: Unfilled sponge can be frozen for 1 month. Place each layer in a freezer bag, seal, label and date. Thaw sponges at room temperature; this will take about 20 minutes. Filled sponge is best eaten immediately.
Variation: Omit jam in the filling and fill cake with cream only. Decorate top with fresh berries and cream swirls.
This sponge mixture can also be baked successfully in a deep, 23 cm round cake tin. Increase the baking time to 40 minutes.
Cut cake horizontally into three layers and fill with the jam and cream, as previously described. You will need to increase the jam to 3/4 cup and the cream to 1 cup.

CITRUS GÉNOISE SPONGE

Preparation time: 40 minutes
Cooking time: 20 minutes
Makes one 20 cm round layer cake

1 cup self-raising flour
4 eggs, lightly beaten
½ cup caster sugar
60 g unsalted butter, melted
   and cooled
2 teaspoons finely grated
   orange rind
1 teaspoon finely grated lemon
   rind

Lemon Curd Filling
6 teaspoons cornflour
⅓ cup caster sugar
¾ cup milk
⅓ cup lemon juice
2 eggs, lightly beaten

▶ PREHEAT OVEN to moderate 180°C. Brush two shallow, 20 cm round sandwich tins with melted butter or oil. Line bases with paper; grease the paper. Dust the tins lightly with flour, shake off excess.

1 Sift the flour three times onto greaseproof paper.
Combine eggs and sugar in medium heatproof mixing bowl. Place bowl over pan of simmering water. Beat

until mixture is thick and pale yellow. Remove from heat, continue to beat until mixture has cooled slightly and increased in volume.

2 Add flour, melted butter, lemon and orange rind. Using metal spoon, fold quickly and lightly until ingredients are just combined.

Spread mixture evenly into prepared tins. Bake for 20 minutes or until the sponges are lightly golden and shrink from sides of tins. Leave sponges in tins for 5 minutes before turning onto wire rack to cool.

3 To make Lemon Curd Filling: Combine cornflour, sugar, milk, lemon juice and eggs in small pan, mix well. Stir over low heat until mixture boils and thickens, cook for 1 minute longer. Remove from heat. Transfer to a small bowl, cover with plastic wrap and allow to cool before using.

4 Cut each cake in half horizontally. Place a cake layer on a serving plate. Spread the cake evenly with the filling. Continue layering with remaining cake and filling, ending with a cake layer on top. Dust the top with sifted icing sugar, if desired.

COOK'S FILE

Storage time: Unfilled sponge can be frozen for 1 month. Place each layer in a freezer bag, seal, label and date. Thaw sponges at room temperature; this will take about 20 minutes. Filled sponge is best eaten immediately.
Variation: Use lemon or orange rind only in cake, if preferred. Orange juice can be used in place of lemon in filling.

VICTORIA SPONGE

Preparation time: 20 minutes
Cooking time: 20 minutes
Makes one 20 cm round layer cake

1 cup self-raising flour
4 eggs, lightly beaten
¾ cup sugar
60 g unsalted butter, melted and cooled
¼ cup warm milk
½ cup raspberry jam
icing sugar, for decoration

➤ PREHEAT OVEN to moderate 180˚C. Brush two shallow, 20 cm round sandwich tins with melted butter or oil. Line bases with paper; grease the paper. Dust the tins lightly with flour, shake off excess.

1 Sift the flour three times onto greaseproof paper.

Using electric beaters, beat eggs in small mixing bowl for 5 minutes or until thick and pale.

2 Add sugar gradually, 1 tablespoon at a time, beating constantly until it has dissolved and the mixture is pale yellow and glossy. Transfer mixture to a large mixing bowl.

Using a metal spoon, fold in butter, milk and flour quickly and lightly.

3 Spread mixture evenly into the prepared tins. Bake for 20 minutes or until sponges are lightly golden and shrink from sides of tins. Leave the sponges in tins for 5 minutes before turning onto wire rack to cool.

Spread jam on both sponge layers, place together. Dust with sifted icing sugar just before serving.

COOK'S FILE

Storage time: Unfilled sponge can be frozen for 1 month. Place each layer in a freezer bag, seal, label and date. Thaw sponges at room temperature; this will take about 20 minutes. Filled sponge is best eaten immediately.
Hint: Spread the jam on both of the cake layers to stop the two halves slipping apart on cutting.

1

2

3

CORNFLOUR SPONGE

Preparation time: 35 minutes
Cooking time: 15 minutes
Makes one 20 cm round layer cake

½ cup cornflour
2 tablespoons self-raising flour
3 eggs, lightly beaten
½ cup caster sugar
⅔ cup cream

Passionfruit Icing
1¼ cups icing sugar
1 teaspoon unsalted butter
¼ cup passionfruit pulp

➤ PREHEAT OVEN to moderate 180°C.
Brush two shallow, 20 cm round sandwich tins with melted butter or oil. Line bases with paper; grease paper. Dust tins lightly with flour, shake off excess.

1 Sift flours three times onto greaseproof paper.
Using electric beaters, beat eggs in small mixing bowl for 5 minutes or until thick and pale.
Add sugar gradually, beating constantly until dissolved and mixture is pale yellow and glossy. Transfer mixture to large mixing bowl.

2 Using a metal spoon, fold in flours quickly and lightly.
Spoon mixture evenly into prepared tins. Bake for 15 minutes or until the sponges are golden and shrink from the sides of the tins. Leave sponges in tins for 5 minutes before turning onto wire rack to cool.

3 Beat cream in medium bowl until stiff peaks form.
Using a flat-bladed knife, spread the cream evenly on one of the sponge layers. Place the other sponge on top.

To make Passionfruit Icing: Combine the sifted icing sugar, butter and sufficient passionfruit pulp in a small bowl to make a stiff paste. Stand bowl in pan of simmering water, stirring until icing is smooth and glossy; remove from heat. Spread over cake using a flat-bladed knife. Allow icing to set before serving cake.

COOK'S FILE

Storage time: Unfilled sponge can be frozen for 1 month. Place each layer in a freezer bag, seal, label and date. Thaw sponges at room temperature; this will take about 20 minutes. Filled sponge is best eaten immediately.

Hint: If any excess icing runs down the side of the cake, leave to set before removing. Simply cut away from the edge; the icing will not have stuck to the side of the cake.

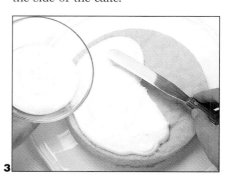

CLASSIC SWISS ROLL

Preparation time: 25 minutes
Cooking time: 10 to 12 minutes
Makes one Swiss roll

¾ cup self-raising flour
3 eggs, lightly beaten
½ cup caster sugar
¼ cup caster sugar, extra
½ cup strawberry jam

➤ PREHEAT OVEN to moderately hot 210°C.

1 Brush a shallow, 30 x 25 x 2 cm Swiss roll tin with melted butter or oil. Line base and two sides with paper; grease paper. Sift flour three times onto greaseproof paper.

Using electric beaters, beat eggs in small mixing bowl for 5 minutes or until thick and pale.

2 Add sugar gradually, beating constantly until dissolved and mixture is pale and glossy. Transfer mixture to large mixing bowl.

Using a metal spoon, fold in flour quickly and lightly.

3 Spread mixture evenly into prepared tin; smooth surface. Bake for 10 to 12 minutes or until lightly golden and springy to the touch.

Turn cake out onto a dry, clean tea-towel covered with greaseproof paper that has been sprinkled with the extra sugar; leave for 1 minute. Using the tea-towel as a guide, carefully roll cake up with the paper; leave for 5 minutes or until cool.

4 Unroll cake, discard paper. Spread with jam; re-roll. Trim ends with knife; decorate as desired.

COOK'S FILE

Storage time: Filled roll is best eaten immediately.

Hint: Jam is best beaten with a spatula for 30 seconds before it is applied to the cake. This will soften the jam and make it easier to spread. Any type of jam can be used.

LAYERED CHOCOLATE SPONGE

Preparation time: 40 minutes
Cooking time: 20 minutes
Makes one 20 cm round layer cake

¾ cup self-raising flour
2 tablespoons cocoa powder
4 eggs, lightly beaten
¾ cup caster sugar

Vienna Cream
125 g unsalted butter
1¼ cups icing sugar
2 tablespoons cocoa powder
2 tablespoons milk

Glacé Icing
1¼ cups icing sugar
1 teaspoon instant coffee
   powder
1 teaspoon unsalted butter,
   melted
1-2 tablespoons water
10 walnut halves

➤ PREHEAT OVEN to moderate 180°C. Brush two shallow, 20 cm round sandwich tins with melted butter or oil. Line bases with paper, grease paper. Dust tins lightly with flour, shake off excess.

1 Sift flour and cocoa three times onto greaseproof paper.
Using electric beaters, beat the eggs in a small mixing bowl for 5 minutes or until thick and pale. Add the sugar gradually, beating constantly until it has dissolved and the mixture is pale yellow and glossy. Transfer mixture to large mixing bowl.

2 Using a metal spoon, fold in sifted ingredients quickly and lightly.
Spoon mixture evenly into prepared tins. Bake for 20 minutes or until the sponges are lightly golden and shrink from sides of tins. Leave the sponges in tins for 5 minutes before turning onto wire rack to cool.

3 **To make Vienna Cream:** Using electric beaters, beat the butter in a small bowl until light and fluffy. Add sifted icing sugar and cocoa, beating for 8 to 10 minutes or until mixture is smooth and fluffy. Add milk and continue beating for 3 minutes.

4 Spread one sponge with half the Vienna Cream. Place remaining cream in a piping bag and pipe rosettes of cream around the edge of the sponge. Place other sponge on top.

5 **To make Glacé Icing:** Combine sifted icing sugar and coffee powder with melted butter and sufficient water to form a firm paste. Stand bowl in pan of simmering water, stirring until icing is smooth and glossy; remove from heat.

6 Spread the icing over cake using a flat-bladed knife. Decorate with the walnut halves. Allow the icing to set before serving.

COOK'S FILE

Storage time: Unfilled sponge can be frozen for 1 month. Place each layer in a freezer bag; seal, label and date. Thaw sponges at room temperature; this will take about 20 minutes. Filled sponge is best eaten immediately.

Hint: Overheating the icing will make it dull, flat and grainy. Work quickly when applying icing, dipping the knife into hot water occasionally to give a smooth, shiny appearance; do not reheat icing.

Some packets of flour carry the label 'ready sifted'. Despite that, all flour should be sifted before use to rid it of any lumps and to incorporate air. The heat of the oven causes the air trapped in the cake mixture to rise. Self-raising flour contains baking powder, which is a raising agent.

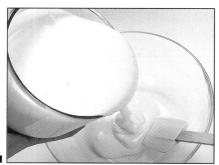

4

5

6

SPONGE WITH MOCK CREAM FILLING

Preparation time: 30 minutes
Cooking time: 15 minutes
Makes one 20 cm round layer cake

¾ cup self-raising flour
3 eggs, lightly beaten
½ cup caster sugar
icing sugar, for decoration

Mock Cream Filling
125 g unsalted butter
½ cup caster sugar
1 teaspoon imitation vanilla
   essence

➤ PREHEAT OVEN to moderate 180°C. Brush two shallow, 20 cm round sandwich tins with melted butter or oil. Line bases with paper; grease paper. Dust the tins with flour, shake off excess.

1 Sift the flour three times onto greaseproof paper. Using electric beaters, beat eggs in a small bowl for 5 minutes or until thick and pale.
Add the sugar gradually, beating constantly until dissolved and mixture is pale yellow and glossy. Transfer the mixture to a large mixing bowl.

2 Using a metal spoon, fold in flour quickly and lightly. Spread mixture evenly into the prepared tins. Bake for 15 minutes or until sponges are lightly golden and shrink from sides of tins. Leave sponges in tins 5 minutes before turning onto wire rack to cool.

3 To make Mock Cream Filling: Using electric beaters, beat butter and sugar in small mixing bowl until light and creamy. Remove bowl from electric mixer. Cover the mixture with cold water, swirl water around and pour off. Beat with electric beaters for a further 2 minutes.
Repeat this whole process six times or until cream is white and fluffy and sugar is dissolved. Stir in essence. Sandwich cakes with filling. Dust with sifted icing sugar just before serving.

COOK'S FILE

Storage time: Unfilled sponge can be frozen for 1 month. Place each layer in a freezer bag, seal, label and date. Thaw sponges at room temperature; this will take about 20 minutes. Filled sponge is best eaten immediately.
Variation: Stir 90 g grated chocolate through the filling mixture.

1

3

SPICED APPLE ROLL

Preparation time: 40 minutes
Cooking time: 12 minutes
Makes one Swiss roll

¾ cup self-raising flour
1 teaspoon five spice powder
3 eggs, lightly beaten
½ cup caster sugar
icing sugar, for decoration

Apple Filling
2 large green apples, peeled
 and cored
1 tablespoon caster sugar
1 teaspoon lemon juice
⅔ cup cream

➤ PREHEAT OVEN to moderately hot 210°C.
Brush a shallow, 30 x 25 x 2 cm Swiss roll tin with melted butter or oil. Line base and two sides with paper; grease the paper.
Sift flour and spice three times onto greaseproof paper.
Using electric beaters, beat eggs in small mixing bowl for 5 minutes or until thick and pale.
1 Add the sugar gradually, beating constantly until dissolved and mixture is pale yellow and glossy. Transfer mixture to large mixing bowl.
Using a metal spoon, fold in the dry ingredients quickly and lightly.
2 Spread the mixture evenly into the prepared tin; smooth the surface. Bake for 10 to 12 minutes or until lightly golden and springy to the touch.
Turn cake out onto a clean, dry tea-towel covered with greaseproof paper; leave for 1 minute.
Using tea-towel as a guide, carefully roll up the cake with the paper; leave for 5 minutes or until cool. Unroll and discard the paper.

3 **To make Apple Filling:** Place apples in small pan, add ¼ cup water and cook on low heat until fruit is tender. Discard any remaining liquid. Use a fork to break up apples, stir in sugar and lemon juice to taste. Cool. Beat cream in small bowl until stiff peaks form. Refrigerate until required. Spread roll with cooled apples and whipped cream; re-roll. Trim ends of roll with serrated knife. Dust with icing sugar just before serving.

COOK'S FILE

Storage time: Filled roll is best eaten immediately.
Hint: This Swiss roll is excellent served as a dessert.

1

2

3

HAZELNUT CHOCOLATE ROLL

Preparation time: 35 minutes
Cooking time: 12 minutes
Makes one Swiss roll

½ cup self-raising flour
3 eggs, lightly beaten
⅓ cup caster sugar
100 g chocolate, finely
   chopped
½ cup ground hazelnut meal
1 tablespoon strong black coffee
1¼ cups cream
1 tablespoon strong black
   coffee, extra
⅓ cup icing sugar
2 tablespoons cocoa powder

➤ PREHEAT OVEN to moderately hot 210°C.
Brush shallow, 30 x 25 x 2 cm Swiss roll tin with melted butter or oil. Line the base and two sides with paper; grease the paper.

1 Sift the flour three times onto greaseproof paper.
Using electric beaters, beat eggs in small mixing bowl for 5 minutes or until thick and pale.
Add sugar gradually, beating constantly until dissolved and mixture is pale yellow and glossy. Transfer to a large mixing bowl.

2 Using a large metal spoon, fold in chocolate, hazelnut meal, coffee liquid and flour quickly and lightly. Spread mixture evenly into the prepared tin; smooth surface. Bake 12 minutes or until golden and springy to the touch. Beat cream and extra coffee liquid in small bowl until stiff peaks form. Refrigerate until required.

3 Turn cake onto a clean, dry tea-towel covered with greaseproof paper which has been dusted evenly with

sifted icing sugar and cocoa; leave for 1 minute. Using tea-towel as a guide, carefully roll up cake with paper; leave cake for 5 minutes or until cool.
Unroll cake, discard paper. Spread with coffee cream filling; re-roll. Trim the ends of roll with a serrated knife.

COOK'S FILE

Storage time: Filled roll is best eaten immediately.
Hint: Make strong black coffee using instant coffee powder or granules or by brewing espresso coffee.

SPONGE FINGERS

Preparation time: 20 minutes
Cooking time: 6 minutes
Makes 24 sponge fingers

⅓ cup self-raising flour
2 tablespoons cornflour
2 eggs, separated
⅓ cup caster sugar
20 g unsalted butter, melted
⅔ cup cream
½ teaspoon imitation vanilla
    essence
icing sugar, for decoration

➤ PREHEAT OVEN to moderate 180°C. Brush two 32 x 28 cm biscuit trays with melted butter or oil, line bases with paper; grease paper. Dust tins lightly with flour, shake off the excess. Mark lines in the flour 7 cm apart on each tray.

1 Sift the flours three times onto greaseproof paper. Place egg whites in a small, clean, dry mixing bowl. Using electric beaters, beat until firm peaks form. Add sugar gradually, beating constantly until dissolved and mixture is glossy and thick.

Add beaten egg yolks, beat a further 20 seconds. Transfer mixture to large mixing bowl. Using a metal spoon fold in flours gradually and lightly. Add butter, fold through.

2 Place mixture in large piping bag fitted with a round nozzle.

Pipe fingers between the 7 cm lines, leaving 5 cm between each one.

Bake for 6 minutes or until lightly golden. Leave sponge fingers on tins for 5 minutes before placing them on wire rack to cool.

3 Beat cream and essence in small bowl until stiff peaks form.

Sandwich two sponge fingers together with a spoonful of whipped cream. Repeat with the remaining fingers and cream. Dust with sifted icing sugar just before serving.

COOK'S FILE

Storage time: Filled fingers are best eaten immediately.

Variation: Spoon mixture into fingers or rounds, instead of using a piping bag. Fold ¼ cup finely chopped strawberries through the whipped cream, if desired.

1

2

3

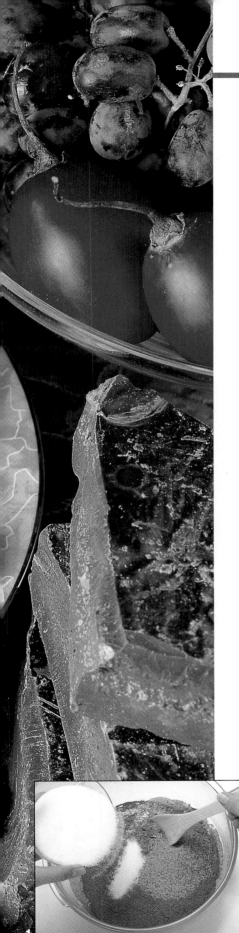

CHOCOLATE CAKES

MOIST CHOCOLATE CAKE WITH CREAMY CHOCOLATE SAUCE

Preparation time: 30 minutes
Cooking time: 35 minutes
Makes one 23 cm ring cake

13/4 cups self-raising flour
1 teaspoon bicarbonate of soda
1/2 cup cocoa powder
1 tablespoon instant coffee
    powder
3/4 cup caster sugar
1/4 cup demerara sugar
2 eggs, lightly beaten
1 teaspoon imitation vanilla
    essence
1 cup buttermilk
1/2 cup milk
60 g unsalted butter, melted

Creamy Chocolate Sauce
100 g dark chocolate, coarsely
    chopped
1/3 cup cream

➤ PREHEAT OVEN to moderate 180°C.

1 Brush a deep, 23 cm fluted ring tin with melted butter or oil. Sift the flour, soda, cocoa and coffee into a large mixing bowl. Add the sugars.

2 Pour combined eggs, liquids and melted butter onto the dry ingredients; using electric beaters, beat the mixture on a low speed for 3 minutes until it is just moistened.

3 Beat the mixture on high speed for 5 minutes or until free of lumps and increased in volume.

Pour mixture evenly into prepared tin; smooth surface. Bake 35 minutes or until skewer comes out clean when inserted in centre of cake. Leave cake in tin 10 minutes before turning onto wire rack to cool.

To make Creamy Chocolate Sauce: Combine chocolate and cream in small pan. Stir over low heat until chocolate melts. Remove from heat. Cool to room temperature. Pour sauce over cake. Serve at once with fresh fruit.

COOK'S FILE

Storage time: 3 days in an airtight container or up to 2 months in the freezer without sauce.

Hint: Store chocolate, wrapped, in a cool place, but not in the refrigerator; if it is too cold, it will acquire a dusty white 'bloom' and be unsuitable for decoration purposes.

BEST EVER CHOCOLATE CAKE

Preparation time: 25 minutes
Cooking time: 45 minutes
Makes one 20 cm square cake

125 g unsalted butter
½ cup caster sugar
⅓ cup icing sugar
2 eggs, lightly beaten
1 teaspoon imitation vanilla
   essence
¼ cup blackberry jam
1¼ cups self-raising flour
½ cup cocoa powder
1 teaspoon bicarbonate of soda
1 cup milk

Rich Chocolate Butter Cream
50 g dark chocolate, finely
   chopped
25 g unsalted butter
¼ cup icing sugar
2 teaspoons cream

➤ PREHEAT OVEN to moderate 180°C. Brush a deep, 20 cm square cake tin with melted butter or oil, line the base and sides with paper; grease the paper.

1 Using electric beaters, beat butter and sugar and sifted icing sugar in small mixing bowl until light and creamy. Add eggs gradually, beating thoroughly after each addition. Add essence and jam; beat until combined.

2 Transfer mixture to large mixing bowl. Using a metal spoon, fold in sifted flour, cocoa and soda alternately with milk. Stir until just combined and the mixture is almost smooth.

Pour mixture into prepared tin; smooth surface. Bake 45 minutes or until skewer comes out clean when inserted in centre. Leave cake 15 minutes before turning onto wire rack to cool.

3 To make the Rich Chocolate Butter Cream: Combine the chocolate, butter, sifted icing sugar and cream in a small pan. Stir over low heat until the mixture is smooth and glossy. Remove from the heat. Spread Butter Cream over top of cake using a flat-bladed knife.

COOK'S FILE

Storage time: 1 week in an airtight container or up to 3 months in the freezer uniced.

Hint: The surface of this cake may be slightly wrinkled after cooking; this is easily concealed by the Butter Cream.

CHOC-RUM AND RAISIN CAKE

Preparation time: 40 minutes
Cooking time: 1 hour
Makes one 20 cm round cake

½ cup raisins, chopped in half
2 tablespoons overproof rum
185 g unsalted butter
¾ cup caster sugar
2 eggs, lightly beaten
2 cups self-raising flour
⅓ cup cocoa powder
¾ cup milk

Choc-Rum Icing
125 g unsalted butter
⅔ cup icing sugar
2-3 tablespoons overproof rum
¼ cup grated dark chocolate

➤ SOAK RAISINS in rum overnight. Preheat oven to moderate 180°C. Brush a deep, 20 cm round cake tin with melted butter or oil, line base and side with paper; grease paper.

1 Using electric beaters, beat butter and sugar in small mixing bowl until light and creamy. Add eggs gradually, beating thoroughly after each addition. Transfer mixture to a large mixing bowl. Using a metal spoon, fold in rum and raisins.

2 Fold in the sifted flour and cocoa alternately with milk. Stir until just combined and mixture is almost smooth.

3 Pour mixture into prepared tin; smooth surface. Bake 1 hour or until skewer comes out clean when inserted in centre of cake. Leave cake in the tin 15 minutes before turning onto wire rack to cool.

To make Choc-Rum Icing: Using electric beaters, beat butter and sifted icing sugar in small mixing bowl until light and creamy. Add rum and chocolate; beat until smooth and fluffy.

4 Spread two-thirds of the icing over top and sides of cake using a flat-bladed knife. Pipe edging around cake rim using remainder of icing. Decorate with purchased chocolates or chocolate decoration of your choice (see page 11).

COOK'S FILE

Storage time: 3 days in an airtight container or up to 2 months in the freezer uniced.

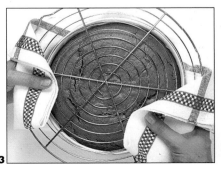

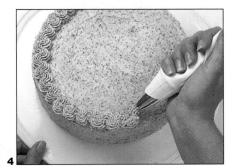

1

2

3

4

MILK CHOCOLATE CHIP CAKE

Preparation time: 25 minutes
Cooking time: 35 minutes
Makes one 20 cm ring cake

90 g unsalted butter
⅓ cup caster sugar
2 eggs, lightly beaten
½ teaspoon imitation vanilla
essence
60 g milk chocolate, coarsely
chopped
½ cup/90 g milk Choc Bits
1¼ cups self-raising flour
extra Choc Bits, for decoration

Milk Chocolate Icing
100 g milk chocolate, coarsely
chopped
¼ cup cream
30 g unsalted butter
2 teaspoons icing sugar

➤ PREHEAT OVEN to moderate 180°C. Brush a deep, 20 cm ring tin with melted butter or oil. Line base with paper; grease paper.

1 Coat base and side evenly with flour; shake off excess.

Using electric beaters, beat butter and sugar in small mixing bowl until light and creamy. Add the eggs gradually, beating thoroughly after each addition. Add essence; beat until combined.

2 Place chocolate in a glass bowl. Stir over barely simmering water until melted; remove from heat. Transfer butter mixture to large mixing bowl; add chocolate and Choc Bits.

3 Using a metal spoon, fold in sifted flour. Stir until just combined and the mixture is almost smooth.

Spoon mixture evenly into prepared tin; smooth surface. Bake 35 minutes or until skewer comes out clean when inserted in centre of cake. Leave cake in tin 10 minutes before turning onto wire rack to cool.

4 To make Milk Chocolate Icing: Combine chocolate, cream, butter and sifted icing sugar in a small pan. Stir over low heat until chocolate and butter have melted and mixture is smooth; remove from heat. Cool. Pour icing over cake. Top with extra Choc Bits.

COOK'S FILE

Storage time: 3 days in an airtight container or up to 2 months in the freezer uniced.

MELT AND MIX CHOCOLATE CAKE

Preparation time: 20 minutes
Cooking time: 1 hour 45 minutes
Makes one 20 cm round cake

1⅓ cups self-raising flour
⅓ cup plain flour
⅓ cup cocoa powder
1 tablespoon instant coffee
    powder
¾ cup caster sugar
¼ cup soft brown sugar
200 g unsalted butter
1 tablespoon golden syrup
½ cup hot water

100 g dark chocolate, coarsely
    chopped
2 eggs, lightly beaten
2 tablespoons cocoa powder
1 tablespoon icing sugar

➤ PREHEAT OVEN to moderately slow 160°C. Brush a deep, 20 cm round cake tin with melted butter or oil, line base and side with paper; grease paper.

1 Sift the flours, cocoa and coffee into a large mixing bowl. Make a well in the centre.

2 Combine sugars, butter, syrup, water and chocolate in a large pan. Stir over a low heat until the butter and chocolate are melted and the sugars dissolved; remove from heat.

3 Add butter mixture to the dry ingredients. Using a whisk, stir until just combined; add the eggs, mix well; do not overbeat.

Pour mixture into prepared tin. Bake for 1 hour 45 minutes or until skewer comes out clean when inserted in centre of cake. Leave cake in tin 1 hour before turning onto wire rack to cool. Dust cake with combined sifted cocoa and icing sugar.

COOK'S FILE

Storage time: 1 week in an airtight container or for up to 3 months stored in the freezer.

Hint: Store all types of sugar in airtight containers away from the light.

1

2

3

DEVIL'S FOOD CAKE

Preparation time: 30 minutes
Cooking time: 40 to 50 minutes
Makes one 20 cm round cake

1⅓ cups plain flour
⅔ cup cocoa powder
1 teaspoon bicarbonate of soda
1 cup caster sugar
2 eggs, lightly beaten
1 cup buttermilk
1 teaspoon imitation vanilla
　essence
125 g unsalted butter, softened
½ cup cream, whipped
60 g white chocolate, coarsely
　chopped

Feathered Icing
60 g unsalted butter
60 g dark chocolate, melted

➤ PREHEAT OVEN to moderate 180°C. Brush a deep, 20 cm round tin with melted butter or oil, line base and side with paper; grease paper.
Sift flour, cocoa and soda into large mixing bowl. Add sugar.
1 Pour the combined eggs, buttermilk, essence and butter onto dry ingredients; using electric beaters, beat on low speed for 3 minutes or until just moistened.
2 Beat the mixture on high speed for 5 minutes or until mixture is free of lumps and increased in volume. Pour mixture into prepared tin; smooth the surface. Bake 40 to 50 minutes or until skewer comes out clean when inserted in centre of cake. Leave cake in tin for 15 minutes before turning onto wire rack to cool.

3 To make the Feathered Icing: Combine butter and chocolate in a small pan; stir over a low heat until melted; remove from heat. Cool. Cut the dome off the cake to level the surface. Cut cake in half horizontally.
Spread whipped cream over half of cake from which dome was sliced. Sandwich with the other layer. Spread icing over top using flat-bladed knife. Place white chocolate in glass bowl. Stir over barely simmering water until melted; remove from heat. Cool slightly.
4 Spoon melted chocolate into a small paper icing bag, seal open end. Snip tip off the piping bag; pipe 8 to 10 small to large circles around the top of the cake. Drag a skewer from the centre circle to the outside of the cake. Clean the skewer and repeat this process, working around the cake in wedges. This is called feathering (see page 11).

COOK'S FILE

Storage time: 3 days unfilled in an airtight container or up to 3 months in the freezer unfilled and uniced. The filled cake is best assembled and eaten the same day.

CHOCOLATE PEANUT FUDGE CAKE

Preparation time: 40 minutes
Cooking time: 1 hour
Makes one 20 cm round cake

1¼ cups self-raising flour
¼ cup cocoa powder
200 g unsalted butter
100 g dark chocolate, coarsely
    chopped
¼ cup smooth peanut butter
¾ cup cream
¾ cup caster sugar
2 eggs, lightly beaten
cocoa powder, for decoration
packaged chocolate-dipped
    peanuts, for decoration

Dark Chocolate Icing
150 g dark chocolate, coarsely
    chopped
90 g unsalted butter
½ cup condensed milk

➤ PREHEAT OVEN to moderate 180°C. Brush a deep, 20 cm round tin with melted butter or oil, line base and side with paper; grease paper.

1 Sift flour and cocoa in a large mixing bowl. Make a well in the centre.
Combine butter, chocolate, peanut butter, cream and sugar in a medium pan. Stir over low heat until butter and chocolate have melted and sugar has dissolved; remove from heat.

2 Add the butter mixture to the dry ingredients. Using a whisk, stir until just combined; add eggs, mix well; do not overbeat.
Pour mixture into prepared tin. Bake for 1 hour or until skewer comes out clean when inserted in centre of cake.

3 Leave cake in tin 30 minutes before turning onto wire rack to cool.

To make Dark Chocolate Icing: Combine chocolate, butter and condensed milk in small pan. Stir over low heat until chocolate and butter melt and mixture is smooth; remove from heat. Cool until thick and spreadable.

4 Cut the cake in half horizontally. Spread half the chocolate mixture over base half of cake. Sandwich with top layer of cake.
Spread rest of icing over top of cake. Sprinkle with extra cocoa powder; decorate with chocolate-dipped peanuts.

COOK'S FILE

Storage time: 3 days in an airtight container or up to 2 months in the freezer uniced.

WHITE CHOCOLATE AND YOGHURT CAKE

Preparation time: 30 minutes
Cooking time: 40 minutes
Makes one 20 cm round cake

125 g unsalted butter
½ cup caster sugar
2 eggs, lightly beaten
1 teaspoon imitation vanilla
   essence
100 g white chocolate, coarsely
   chopped
½ cup plain or vanilla yoghurt
1½ cups self-raising flour

White Chocolate Topping
125 g cream cheese, softened
60 g white chocolate, melted
2 tablespoons plain yoghurt

➤ PREHEAT OVEN to moderate 180°C. Brush a deep, 20 cm round cake tin with melted butter or oil, line base and side with paper; grease paper.

1 Using electric beaters, beat butter and sugar in small mixing bowl until light and creamy. Add eggs gradually, beating thoroughly after each addition. Add essence; beat until combined.

2 Place chocolate in glass bowl. Stir over barely simmering water until melted; remove from heat.

Transfer butter mixture to large mixing bowl; add chocolate and yoghurt. Using a metal spoon, fold in sifted flour. Stir until just combined and the mixture is almost smooth.

3 Pour mixture into prepared tin; smooth surface.

Bake 40 minutes or until skewer comes out clean when inserted in centre of cake. Stand cake in tin 15 minutes

before turning onto wire rack to cool.

To make the White Chocolate Topping: Using electric beaters, beat cream cheese in small mixing bowl until light and creamy. Add chocolate and yoghurt, beating 5 minutes or until mixture is smooth and fluffy. Spread icing completely over cake using a flat-bladed knife. Decorate cake with white chocolate curls (refer to page 11).

COOK'S FILE

Storage time: 3 days in an airtight container or up to 1 month in the freezer uniced.

Variation: To make a more moist, heavier cake, use ⅔ cup yoghurt. This cake can also be made with a flavoured yoghurt. Substitute vanilla yoghurt for the plain in the White Chocolate Topping.

1

2

3

CHOCOLATE SPICE CAKE

Preparation time: 40 minutes
Cooking time: 45 minutes
Makes one 20 cm round cake

100 g unsalted butter
2/3 cup caster sugar
2 eggs, lightly beaten
1 tablespoon golden syrup
1½ cups self-raising flour
¼ cup cocoa powder
½ teaspoon bicarbonate
 of soda
¼ teaspoon ground cloves
¼ teaspoon ground allspice
2/3 cup milk

Spicy Syrup
½ cup caster sugar
2/3 cup water
¼ teaspoon ground cloves
¼ teaspoon ground allspice

➤ PREHEAT OVEN to moderate 180°C. Brush a deep, 20 cm round cake tin with melted butter or oil, line base and side with paper; grease paper.

1 Using electric beaters, beat butter and sugar in small mixing bowl until light and creamy. Add eggs gradually, beating thoroughly after each addition. Add syrup; beat until combined.

2 Transfer the mixture to a large mixing bowl. Using a metal spoon, fold in the sifted flour, cocoa, soda and spices alternately with milk.

Stir until just combined and mixture is almost smooth. Pour mixture into prepared tin; smooth surface. Bake for 45 minutes or until skewer comes out clean when inserted in centre of cake. Leave cake in tin to cool.

3 To make Spicy Syrup: Combine sugar, water and spices in small pan. Stir constantly over low heat until mixture boils and sugar has dissolved.

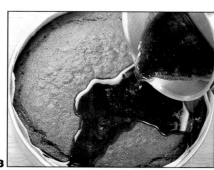

Reduce heat, simmer without stirring, uncovered, until mixture has thickened and reduced by half. Remove from heat; leave until bubbles subside.

Pour the hot Spicy Syrup mixture over the cake while it is still in the tin. When all the syrup has been absorbed, turn cake out of tin.

COOK'S FILE

Storage time: 3 days in an airtight container or up to 2 months in the freezer without syrup.

Hint: Keep ground spices in airtight jars away from direct sunlight or their flavour will quickly deteriorate.

CHERRY CHOCOLATE RING

Preparation time: 10 minutes
Cooking time: 45 minutes
Makes one 23 cm ring cake

250 g unsalted butter
1 cup caster sugar
3 eggs, lightly beaten
1 cup/200 g halved glacé cherries
⅓ cup Choc Bits
2 cups plain flour
½ teaspoon bicarbonate of soda
125 g dark chocolate, coarsely chopped, optional
2 teaspoons oil, optional
whipped cream and glacé cherries, for decoration

➤ PREHEAT OVEN to moderate 180°C. Brush a deep, 23 cm fluted ring tin with melted butter or oil. Coat base and side evenly with flour; shake off the excess.

1 Using electric beaters, beat butter and sugar in a small mixing bowl until creamy and white. Add the eggs gradually, beating thoroughly after each addition.

2 Transfer mixture to large mixing bowl; add cherries and Choc Bits. Using a metal spoon, fold in sifted flour and soda. Stir until just combined and mixture is almost smooth.

Spoon mixture evenly into prepared tin; smooth the surface. Bake cake for 45 minutes or until skewer comes out clean when inserted in centre.

3 Leave cake in tin 5 minutes before turning out onto wire rack to cool.

Place chocolate and oil in a small heatproof bowl. Stand the bowl over a pan of simmering water, stir until the chocolate has melted and mixture is smooth. Cool slightly.

Spread cake evenly with the melted chocolate mixture using a flat-bladed knife; alternatively, pour the mixture over. Refrigerate the cake, uncovered, for 10 minutes or until the chocolate is firm. Decorate with whipped cream and glacé cherries.

The chocolate topping is optional. This cake can also be covered with whipped cream and decorated with glacé cherries.

COOK'S FILE

Storage time: 3 days in an airtight container or up to 2 months in the freezer uniced.

ESPRESSO CHOCOLATE CAKE WITH LIQUEUR SAUCE

Preparation time: 45 minutes
Cooking time: 30 minutes
Makes one 20 cm baba cake

¼ cup finely ground espresso
  coffee
¾ cup boiling water
150 g unsalted butter
¾ cup soft dark brown sugar
2 eggs, lightly beaten
⅓ cup ground almonds
1½ cups self-raising flour
¼ cup cocoa powder

Chocolate Liqueur Sauce
¾ cup caster sugar
¾ cup water
¼ cup chocolate liqueur

➤ COMBINE COFFEE and water in a small heatproof bowl. Allow to stand 10 minutes. Strain, reserving ½ cup of the liquid.

1 Preheat oven to moderate 180°C. Brush a deep, 20 cm baba tin with melted butter or oil.
Using electric beaters, beat butter and sugar in small mixing bowl until light and creamy. Add eggs gradually, beating thoroughly after each addition.

2 Transfer mixture to large mixing bowl; add almonds. Using a metal spoon, fold in sifted flour and cocoa alternately with strained coffee. Stir until just combined and the mixture is almost smooth.

3 Spoon mixture into prepared tin; smooth surface. Bake 30 minutes or until skewer comes out clean when inserted in centre of cake. Leave cake in tin 15 minutes before turning onto wire rack.

4 To make Chocolate Liqueur Sauce: Combine the sugar, water and liqueur in a small pan.
Stir constantly over low heat until mixture boils and sugar has dissolved. Reduce heat, simmer without stirring, uncovered, until mixture begins to thicken and liquid is reduced by half. Remove from heat, leave the sauce for 2 minutes for the bubbles to subside. Pour sauce into heatproof serving jug. Serve sauce warm with warm cake and pouring cream.

COOK'S FILE

Storage time: This cake is best eaten the day it is made.
Variation: Substitute a coffee liqueur for the chocolate one, if preferred.
Hint: The darker the sugar, the more likely it is to become hard; this is because the film of molasses covering it contains moisture which hardens if it dries. A slice of apple placed in the jar will help to prevent this happening.

CHOCOLATE ORANGE CAKE

Preparation time: 35 minutes
Cooking time: 45 minutes
Makes one 20 cm square cake

180 g unsalted butter
½ cup caster sugar
2 eggs, lightly beaten
1 teaspoon finely grated orange
    rind
¼ cup demerara sugar
½ cup orange juice
2 cups self-raising flour
⅓ cup cocoa powder
orange segments and strips of
    rind, for decoration

Orange Topping
250 g cream cheese, softened
¼ cup icing sugar
1 teaspoon finely grated orange
    rind
⅓ cup orange juice

➤ PREHEAT OVEN to moderate 180°C. Brush a deep, 20 cm square cake tin with melted butter or oil, line base and sides with paper; grease paper.

1 Using electric beaters, beat butter and sugar in small mixing bowl until light and creamy. Add eggs gradually, beating thoroughly after each addition. Add rind; beat until combined.

2 Combine demerara sugar and orange juice in a small pan. Stir over a low heat until sugar has dissolved. Remove from heat.

3 Transfer butter mixture to large mixing bowl. Using a metal spoon, fold in the sifted flour and cocoa alternately with the juice mixture. Stir until just combined and mixture is almost smooth.

Pour mixture into prepared tin; smooth surface. Bake 45 minutes or until skewer comes out clean when inserted in centre of cake. Leave cake in tin 10 minutes before turning onto wire rack to cool.

4 To make Orange Topping: Beat cream cheese in small mixing bowl until light and creamy. Add sifted icing sugar, rind and juice, beating 5 minutes or until mixture is smooth and fluffy. Cut cake in half horizontally. Spread one third of icing mixture over base half. Sandwich with top layer of cake. Spread remaining icing to completely cover cake. Decorate cake with orange segments and thin strips of rind.

COOK'S FILE

Storage time: 3 days in an airtight container or up to 2 months in the freezer uniced.

1

2

3

4

RICH CHOCOLATE MUD CAKE

Preparation time: 20 minutes
Cooking time: 2 hours
Makes one 20 cm round cake

1½ cups self-raising flour
½ cup plain flour
⅓ cup cocoa powder
1 tablespoon instant coffee
  powder
250 g unsalted butter
200 g dark chocolate, coarsely
  chopped
1 tablespoon oil
1 cup water
1½ cups caster sugar
2 eggs, lightly beaten

Chocolate Topping
100 g unsalted butter
100 g dark chocolate, chopped

➤ PREHEAT OVEN to moderately slow 160°C. Brush a deep, 20 cm round cake tin with melted butter or oil, line the base and the side with paper; grease paper.

1 Sift the dry ingredients into a large mixing bowl. Make a well in the centre.
Combine butter, chocolate, oil, water and sugar in a medium pan. Stir over low heat until butter and chocolate have melted and sugar has dissolved. Remove from heat.

2 Add butter mixture to the dry ingredients. Stir with a whisk until just combined; add the eggs, mix well; do not overbeat.

3 Pour mixture into prepared tin. Bake 2 hours or until skewer comes out clean when inserted in centre of cake. Leave cake in tin until cold before turning onto wire rack.

4 To make Chocolate Topping: Combine butter and chocolate in a medium pan. Stir over low heat until butter and chocolate have melted and mixture is smooth. Remove from heat. Allow mixture to cool until it becomes spreadable. Spread icing to completely cover cake. Serve wedges of cake with a dollop of crème fraîche, if desired.

COOK'S FILE

Storage time: 2 weeks in an airtight container stored in a cool place or up to 3 months in the freezer uniced.
Variation: Halve the quantity of Chocolate Topping ingredients if you wish to cover the top of the cake only, as shown in the main picture.
Hint: It is important to allow this cake to become cold before turning it out of the tin. If it is hot, it will break apart.

BUTTER CAKES

BASIC BUTTER CAKE

Preparation time: 20 minutes
Cooking time: 45 minutes
Makes one 20 cm round cake

125 g unsalted butter
¾ cup caster sugar
2 eggs, lightly beaten
1 teaspoon imitation vanilla
  essence
2 cups self-raising flour
½ cup milk

Lemon Glacé Icing
1 cup icing sugar
15 g unsalted butter, melted
3-4 teaspoons lemon juice

➤ PREHEAT OVEN to moderate 180°C. Brush a deep, 20 cm round cake tin with melted butter or oil, line base and side with paper; grease paper.

1 Using electric beaters, beat butter and sugar in small mixing bowl until light and creamy.
Add the eggs gradually, beating thoroughly after each addition. Add essence; beat until combined.

2 Transfer the mixture to a large mixing bowl. Using a metal spoon, fold in the sifted flour alternately with the milk. Stir until just combined and the mixture is almost smooth.
Spoon mixture into prepared tin; smooth surface. Bake 45 minutes or until skewer comes out clean when inserted in centre of cake. Leave in tin 10 minutes before turning onto wire rack to cool.

3 To make Lemon Glacé Icing: Combine sifted icing sugar, melted butter and sufficient lemon juice in a small bowl to form a firm paste.
Stand bowl in a pan of simmering water, stirring until icing is smooth and glossy; do not overheat or the icing will be dull and grainy. Remove from heat. Spread icing over cake using a flat-bladed knife.

COOK'S FILE

Storage time: 1 week in an airtight container or up to 3 months in the freezer uniced.
Variation: Add 1 teaspoon lemon rind and 2 teaspoons lemon juice to cake mixture after adding essence.
Hint: Sugar assists in incorporating air into fat, so it is important to use the type of sugar appropriate to the recipe. Caster sugar is ideal for butter cakes because it is superfine; the finer the crystals, the more numerous the air cells and the lighter the finished cake.

RICH BUTTER CAKE

Preparation time: 20 minutes
Cooking time: 45 minutes
Makes one 20 cm round cake

185 g unsalted butter
¾ cup caster sugar
3 eggs, lightly beaten
1 teaspoon imitation vanilla
   essence
1½ cups self-raising flour
½ cup plain flour
¼ cup milk
icing sugar, for decoration

➤ PREHEAT OVEN to moderate 180°C.
Brush a deep, 20 cm round cake tin with melted butter or oil, line base and side with paper; grease paper.

1 Using electric beaters, beat butter and sugar in small mixing bowl until light and creamy.
Add eggs gradually, beating mixture thoroughly after each addition. Add essence; beat until combined.

2 Transfer mixture to large mixing bowl. Using a metal spoon, fold in sifted flours alternately with milk. Stir until ingredients are just combined and the mixture is almost smooth.

3 Spoon mixture into prepared tin; smooth surface. Bake for 45 minutes or until skewer comes out clean when inserted in centre of cake.
Leave in tin 10 minutes before turning onto wire rack to cool. Dust cake with sifted icing sugar.

COOK'S FILE

Storage time: 1 week in an airtight container or up to 3 months in the freezer uniced.

Hint: If the top of the cake has risen to a peak, or 'tunnels' are visible when you cut it, your oven may be too hot or you may have overmixed the batter.

CHERRY CAKE

Preparation time: 30 minutes
Cooking time: 35 to 40 minutes
Makes one 20 cm ring cake

125 g unsalted butter
¾ cup caster sugar
2 eggs, lightly beaten
½ teaspoon imitation vanilla
   essence
1 cup/265 g glacé cherries,
   chopped
2 cups self-raising flour
½ cup milk

➤ PREHEAT OVEN to moderate
180°C.

1 Brush a deep, 20 cm ring tin with
melted butter or oil, line base with
paper; grease paper. Using electric
beaters, beat butter and sugar in small
bowl until light and creamy.

2 Add eggs gradually, beating
thoroughly after each addition. Add
essence; beat until combined. Transfer
mixture to large mixing bowl; add
cherries. Using a metal spoon, fold in
sifted flour alternately with milk. Stir
until just combined and mixture is
almost smooth.

3 Spoon the mixture evenly into the
prepared tin; smooth surface. Bake for
35 to 40 minutes or until skewer comes
out clean when inserted in centre of
cake. Leave cake in tin 10 minutes
before turning onto wire rack to cool.
Dust with sifted icing sugar, if desired.

COOK'S FILE

Storage time: 1 week in an airtight
container; up to 2 months in the freezer.
Variation: Add ¾ cup canned pitted
cherries, chopped, in place of glacé.
Reduce milk to ⅓ cup. Storage time
will be only 3 days because of the
extra moisture content of the cherries.

SULTANA BARS

Preparation time: 20 minutes
Cooking time: 20 minutes
Makes two bar cakes

125 g unsalted butter
2/3 cup caster sugar
2 eggs, lightly beaten
1/2 teaspoon imitation vanilla
  essence
1 teaspoon brandy (optional)
3/4 cup sultanas or mixed fruit
1 3/4 cups self-raising flour
1/3 cup milk

➤ PREHEAT OVEN to moderate 180°C.
1 Brush two 26 x 8 x 4.5 cm bar tins with melted butter or oil, line base and sides with paper; grease paper.
Using electric beaters, beat butter and sugar in small mixing bowl until light and creamy.
2 Add eggs gradually, beating thoroughly after each addition. Add the essence and brandy, if used; beat until combined.
Transfer mixture to large mixing bowl; add sultanas. Using a metal spoon, fold in sifted flour alternately with the milk. Stir until the ingredients are just combined and the mixture is almost smooth.
3 Spoon mixture evenly into prepared tins; smooth surface. Bake 20 minutes or until skewer comes out clean when inserted in centre of cakes.
Leave the cakes in tins for 5 minutes before turning them onto a wire rack to cool.

COOK'S FILE

Storage time: 1 week in an airtight container or up to 3 months in freezer.
Hint: Break each egg separately into a bowl to check that it is fresh before combining it with others.

COFFEE BUTTER CAKE

Preparation time: 30 minutes
Cooking time: 35 minutes
Makes one 28 cm oblong cake

150 g unsalted butter
1 cup soft brown sugar
2 eggs, lightly beaten
2 teaspoons instant coffee
  powder
2 cups self-raising flour
1/2 cup milk

Coffee Butter Cream
100 g unsalted butter
3/4 cup icing sugar
2 tablespoons soft brown sugar
2 teaspoons instant coffee powder

➤ PREHEAT OVEN to moderate 180°C. Brush a shallow, 28 x 18 x 3 cm oblong cake tin with melted butter or oil, line base and sides with paper; grease paper.
1 Using electric beaters, beat butter and sugar in small mixing bowl until light and creamy. Add eggs gradually, beating thoroughly after each addition. Add coffee powder; beat until combined. Transfer mixture to large mixing bowl.
2 Using a metal spoon, fold in sifted flour alternately with milk. Stir until just combined and mixture is almost smooth. Pour the mixture evenly into prepared tin; smooth surface. Bake for 35 minutes or until skewer comes out clean when inserted in centre of cake. Leave cake in tin 10 minutes before turning onto wire rack to cool.
3 To make Coffee Butter Cream: Using electric beaters, beat butter in small mixing bowl until light and creamy.
Add sifted icing sugar, brown sugar and coffee powder; beat until mixture is smooth and fluffy. Spread mixture over cake using a flat-bladed knife.

COOK'S FILE

Storage time: 4 days in an airtight container or up to 3 months in the freezer uniced.
Variation: Use cocoa powder in the cake and butter cream, if preferred.

*Opposite: Sultana Bars (top),
Coffee Butter Cake (bottom).*

APPLE CRUMBLE CAKE

Preparation time: 45 minutes
Cooking time: 45 minutes
Makes one 23 cm oblong cake

100 g unsalted butter
½ cup caster sugar
1 egg, lightly beaten
½ teaspoon imitation vanilla
  essence
1¼ cups self-raising flour
⅓ cup milk
1 x 425 g can pie apple,
  roughly chopped
2 tablespoons soft brown sugar
40 g unsalted butter, extra
½ cup rolled oats

➤ PREHEAT OVEN to moderate 180°C. Brush a deep, 23 x 13 x 7 cm loaf tin with melted butter or oil, line base and sides with paper; grease the paper.

1 Using electric beaters, beat butter and sugar in a small mixing bowl until light and creamy. Add egg gradually, beating thoroughly after each addition. Add the essence; beat until combined. Transfer the mixture to a large mixing bowl.

2 Using a metal spoon, fold in sifted flour alternately with milk. Stir until just combined and mixture is almost smooth. Spoon mixture into prepared tin; smooth surface. Top with apple. Combine sugar, extra butter and oats in a small pan. Stir over low heat until sugar has dissolved and butter has melted; remove from heat. Spoon crumble evenly over apple.

3 Bake 45 minutes or until skewer comes out clean when inserted in centre of cake.

Leave cake in tin 15 minutes. Place tin on board. Lift cake out by holding greaseproof paper. Transfer cake to wire rack to cool. Tilt cake to one side, pull away half the paper, repeat with other side. Serve plain or with cream.

COOK'S FILE

Storage time: This cake is best eaten the day it is made.
Variation: Use canned pears in place of apple. Substitute breadcrumbs for the rolled oats.

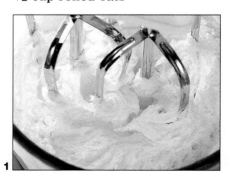

1

2

3

CHOCOLATE AND STRAWBERRY MARBLE CAKE

Preparation time: 30 minutes
Cooking time: 35 minutes
Makes one 28 cm oblong cake

150 g unsalted butter
¾ cup caster sugar
2 eggs, lightly beaten
1 teaspoon imitation vanilla essence
1⅔ cups self-raising flour
½ cup milk
2 tablespoons cocoa powder
4-5 drops red food colouring
4 drops strawberry-flavoured imitation essence or oil

Cream Cheese Icing
100 g cream cheese, softened
¾ cup icing sugar
1 tablespoon hot milk
1 tablespoon cocoa powder

➤ PREHEAT OVEN to moderate 180°C. Brush a shallow, 28 x 18 x 3 cm oblong cake tin with melted butter or oil, line base and sides with paper; grease paper.

1 Using electric beaters, beat butter and sugar in small mixing bowl until light and creamy. Add eggs gradually, beating thoroughly after each addition. Add essence; beat until combined.

2 Transfer mixture to large mixing bowl. Using a metal spoon, fold in sifted flour alternately with milk. Stir until just combined and the mixture is almost smooth. Divide mixture evenly between two bowls. Add the sifted cocoa powder to one bowl and the colouring and flavoured essence to the other; mix well.

3 Spoon the two mixtures alternately into prepared tin. Swirl mixture in circles with skewer. Bake cake for 35 minutes or until skewer comes out clean when inserted in centre. Leave cake in tin 10 minutes before turning onto wire rack to cool.

To make Cream Cheese Icing: Using electric beaters, beat cream cheese and sifted icing sugar in a small mixing bowl until light and creamy. Combine the milk and cocoa powder in a small bowl to form a smooth paste. Add cocoa mixture to the cream cheese mixture. Beat until smooth and fluffy. This icing is best used on the day that it is made. Spread over cake using a flat-bladed knife. Cut the cake into squares to serve.

COOK'S FILE

Storage time: 1 week uniced in an airtight container or up to 3 months in the freezer uniced.

Hint: It is not essential to sift cocoa when it is to be mixed with a liquid.

1

2

3

GINGER BUTTER CAKE

Preparation time: 25 minutes
Cooking time: 45 minutes
Makes one 20 cm round cake

125 g unsalted butter
1/2 cup soft brown sugar
1/4 cup caster sugar
2 eggs, lightly beaten
1¾ cups self-raising flour
1 tablespoon ground ginger
1/2 teaspoon ground cinnamon
1/4 teaspoon ground allspice
1/4 cup malted milk powder
1/2 cup ginger beer
glacé or crystallised ginger, for
    decoration

Ginger Lemon Glacé Icing
1/3 cup icing sugar
1/2 teaspoon ground ginger
20 g unsalted butter, melted
2 teaspoons milk
1 teaspoon lemon juice

➤ PREHEAT OVEN to moderate
180°C.

1 Brush a deep, 20 cm round cake tin
with melted butter or oil, line base and
side with paper; grease paper.
Using electric beaters, beat butter and
sugars in small mixing bowl until light
and creamy. Add the eggs gradually,
beating thoroughly after each addition.

2 Transfer mixture to a large mixing
bowl. Using a metal spoon, fold in the
sifted dry ingredients alternately with
the ginger beer. Stir until just combined and the mixture is almost
smooth.

3 Pour mixture into prepared tin;
smooth surface. Bake 45 minutes or
until a skewer comes out clean when
inserted in centre of cake. Leave cake
in tin 10 minutes before turning onto
wire rack to cool.

**4 To make Ginger Lemon Glacé
Icing:** Combine sifted icing sugar,
ginger, melted butter, milk and lemon
juice in a small bowl to form a paste.
Stand bowl in a pan of simmering
water, stirring until icing is smooth
and glossy; remove from heat.
Spread icing over cake using a flat-
bladed knife. Work quickly, dipping
the knife into hot water occasionally to
give a smooth, shiny finish; do not
reheat icing. Decorate cake with slices
of glacé or crystallised ginger.

COOK'S FILE

Storage time: 1 week in an airtight
container or up to 3 months in the
freezer uniced.

Hint: Glacé fruit is made by soaking
fruit pieces repeatedly in hot syrup,
then coating with a sugar glaze that
becomes flaky when dry. Crystallised
fruits are also dipped in hot syrup, but
are coated in caster sugar to finish.

SAND CAKE

Preparation time: 20 minutes
Cooking time: 45 to 50 minutes
Makes one 23 cm oblong cake

250 g unsalted butter
¾ cup caster sugar
3 eggs, lightly beaten
1 teaspoon imitation vanilla
  essence
2 tablespoons brandy or sherry
1¼ cups self-raising flour
⅔ cup rice flour

➤ PREHEAT OVEN to moderate 180°C. Brush a deep, 23 x 13 x 7 cm loaf tin with melted butter or oil, line base and sides with paper; grease the paper.

1 Using electric beaters, beat butter and sugar in small mixing bowl until light and creamy. Add eggs gradually, beating thoroughly after each addition. Add essence and brandy; beat until combined.

2 Transfer the mixture to a large mixing bowl. Using a metal spoon, fold in sifted flours. Stir until just combined and the mixture is almost smooth. Spoon the mixture into the prepared tin; smooth the surface.

3 Bake for 45 to 50 minutes or until skewer comes out clean when inserted in centre of cake.

Leave cake in tin 10 minutes before turning onto wire rack to cool. Dust with sifted icing sugar, if desired.

COOK'S FILE

Storage time: 3 days in an airtight container or up to 2 months in the freezer.

Variation: Stir 2 tablespoons of lime, lemon, orange or apple juice into the cake mixture in place of the brandy or sherry, if preferred.

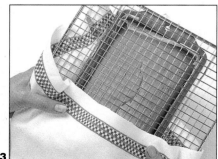

FAIRY CAKES

Preparation time: 30 minutes
Cooking time: 10 to 15 minutes
Makes 36 patty cakes

150 g unsalted butter
¾ cup caster sugar
2 eggs, lightly beaten
1 teaspoon imitation vanilla
　essence
2 teaspoons lemon juice
2 cups self-raising flour
½ cup milk
½ cup raspberry jam
1¼ cups cream, whipped
icing sugar, for decoration

➤ PREHEAT OVEN to moderate
180°C.
1 Line two 12 cup, deep patty tins
with paper patty cases.

Using electric beaters, beat butter and
sugar in small mixing bowl until light
and creamy. Add the eggs gradually,
beating thoroughly after each addition.
Add the essence and juice; beat until
combined.
2 Transfer mixture to large mixing
bowl. Using a metal spoon, fold in
sifted flour alternately with milk. Stir
until just combined and the mixture is
almost smooth.
Spoon level tablespoonfuls of mixture
into prepared patty cases. Bake 10 to
15 minutes or until golden. Leave in
tins 5 minutes before placing on wire
rack to cool.
3 Line tins again with patty cases;
repeat the cooking procedure with the
remaining mixture.
When patty cakes are cold, cut out a
small circle from the top of each one,
cutting down to a depth of about 2 cm
to allow for the filling.

4 Spoon ½ teaspoon jam into each
patty cake; top with 1 teaspoon cream.
Place small circle of cake on top. Dust
with sifted icing sugar.

COOK'S FILE

Storage time: 1 week in an airtight
container without the filling or up to
3 months in the freezer unfilled.
Variation: Add ½ cup grated chocolate
to the cake mix when folding in the flour
and the milk.

CARAMEL CREAM CAKE

Preparation time: 30 minutes
Cooking time: 20 minutes
Makes one 20 cm round layer cake

185 g unsalted butter
½ cup soft brown sugar
2 eggs, lightly beaten
¼ cup caramel corn syrup
2 cups self-raising flour
⅓ cup milk

Caramel Cream
¼ cup soft brown sugar
2 tablespoons water
¾ cup cream, whipped
¼ cup flaked almonds, toasted

➤ PREHEAT OVEN to moderate 180°C. Brush two shallow, 20 cm round cake tins with melted butter or oil, line bases and sides with paper; grease paper.

1 Using electric beaters, beat butter and sugar in small mixing bowl until light and creamy. Add eggs gradually, beating thoroughly after each addition. Add the corn syrup and beat until combined.
Transfer mixture to large mixing bowl. Using a metal spoon, stir in sifted flour alternately with milk. Stir until just combined and the mixture is almost smooth.

2 Divide mixture evenly between the two tins. Smooth the surface. Bake for 20 minutes or until skewer comes out clean when inserted in centre of cakes. Leave in tins 5 minutes before turning onto wire rack to cool.

3 To make the Caramel Cream: Combine sugar and water in a small pan. Stir over low heat until sugar has dissolved. Bring to boil. Reduce heat; simmer until liquid has reduced by half. Remove from heat. Cool slightly.

Allow bubbles to subside. Combine cream and sugar mixture in a small bowl. Cover and chill 10 to 15 minutes. Divide cream in half. Spread the base of one cake with cream. Place other cake on top, spread top with remaining cream, sprinkle with almonds.

COOK'S FILE

Storage time: This cake is best prepared and eaten the same day.
Hint: Caramel corn syrup can be bought in your local supermarket in the cake-making section.

ORANGE SYRUP BUTTER CAKE

Preparation time: 45 minutes
Cooking time: 40 minutes
Makes one 20 cm baba cake

150 g unsalted butter
¾ cup caster sugar
2 eggs, lightly beaten
1 teaspoon finely grated orange
  rind
2 cups self-raising flour
¼ cup powdered milk
½ cup orange juice

Orange Syrup
rind of 1 orange
½ cup orange juice
¼ cup caster sugar

➤ PREHEAT OVEN to moderate 180°C.

1 Brush a deep, 20 cm baba tin with melted butter or oil.
Using electric beaters, beat butter and sugar in small mixing bowl until light and creamy. Add eggs gradually, beating thoroughly after each addition. Add rind; beat until combined.

2 Transfer mixture to a large mixing bowl. Using a metal spoon, fold in the sifted dry ingredients alternately with the juice. Stir until just combined and the mixture is almost smooth.
Spoon mixture into prepared tin; smooth surface. Bake 40 minutes or until a skewer comes out clean when inserted in centre of cake. Leave cake in tin 10 minutes before turning onto wire rack to cool.

3 To make Orange Syrup: Slice orange rind into long, thin strips. Combine juice, sugar and rind in small pan. Stir constantly over low heat until the mixture boils and sugar has dissolved. Reduce heat, simmer without stirring, uncovered, for 15 minutes or until reduced by one quarter.

4 Remove from heat. Pour the warm syrup over the warm cake. Serve with freshly whipped cream, if desired.

COOK'S FILE

Storage time: 3 days in an airtight container or 1 month in the freezer.
Hint: 2 medium oranges were used to produce the 1 cup of juice required in the cake and the syrup in this recipe.

1

2

3

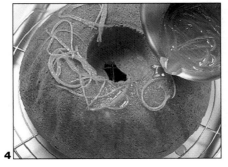

4

CHOCOLATE BUTTER CAKE

Preparation time: 25 minutes
Cooking time: 45 minutes
Makes one 20 cm round cake

150 g unsalted butter
¾ cup caster sugar
2 eggs, lightly beaten
1 teaspoon imitation vanilla
    essence
1¾ cups self-raising flour
½ cup cocoa powder
¾ cup milk
fresh strawberries, for
    decoration

Chocolate Butter Cream
60 g unsalted butter
⅔ cup icing sugar
2 tablespoons cocoa powder
2 teaspoons milk

➤ PREHEAT OVEN to moderate 180°C. Brush a deep, 20 cm round cake tin with melted butter or oil, line base and side with paper; grease paper.

1 Using electric beaters, beat butter and sugar in small mixing bowl until light and creamy. Add the eggs gradually, beating thoroughly after each addition. Add the essence; beat until combined. Transfer mixture to a large mixing bowl.

2 Using a metal spoon, fold in sifted flour and cocoa powder alternately with milk. Stir until just combined and mixture is almost smooth. Spoon the mixture into the prepared tin; smooth the surface.

3 Bake 45 minutes or until skewer comes out clean when inserted in centre of cake. Leave in tin 10 minutes before turning onto wire rack to cool.

4 To make Chocolate Butter Cream: Beat butter in small mixing bowl until light and creamy. Add sifted

icing sugar, cocoa powder and milk, beating 3 minutes or until mixture is smooth and fluffy. Spread icing over cake using a flat-bladed knife. Decorate cake with sliced fresh strawberries.

COOK'S FILE

Storage time: 1 week in an airtight container or up to 3 months in the freezer uniced.

Variation: Use seasonal fruits of your choice for decoration.

PECAN BUTTER CAKE

Preparation time: 25 minutes
Cooking time: 40 minutes
Makes one 20 cm square cake

125 g unsalted butter
½ cup caster sugar
¼ cup raw sugar
2 eggs, lightly beaten
1 teaspoon imitation vanilla
  essence
¾ cup ground pecans
1½ cups self-raising flour
½ cup milk
whole pecans, for decoration

Coffee Icing
1 cup icing sugar
1 teaspoon instant coffee
  powder
1-2 tablespoons water

➤ PREHEAT OVEN to moderate 180°C. Brush a deep, 20 cm square cake tin with melted butter or oil, line base and sides with paper; grease the paper.

1 Using electric beaters, beat butter and sugars in small mixing bowl until light and creamy. Add eggs gradually, beating thoroughly after each addition. Add essence; beat until combined. Transfer mixture to large mixing bowl; add ground pecans.

2 Using a metal spoon, fold in sifted flour alternately with the milk. Stir until just combined and the mixture is almost smooth.

Pour mixture into prepared tin; smooth surface. Bake 40 minutes or until skewer comes out clean when inserted in centre of cake. Leave cake in tin 10 minutes before turning onto wire rack to cool.

3 To make Coffee Icing: Combine sifted icing sugar, coffee and sufficient

liquid in a small bowl to form a firm paste. Stand bowl in pan of simmering water, stirring until icing is smooth and glossy; remove from heat. Spread icing over cake using a flat-bladed knife. Decorate with whole pecans.

Storage time: 1 week in an airtight container or up to 3 months in the freezer uniced.
Variation: Use nuts of your choice.

FRUIT AND VEGETABLE CAKES

ZUCCHINI AND RAISIN CAKE

Preparation time: 15 minutes
Cooking time: 35 to 40 minutes
Makes one 20 cm baba cake

125 g unsalted butter
2/3 cup caster sugar
2 eggs, lightly beaten
2 teaspoons imitation vanilla
   essence
1 1/2 cups coarsely grated
   zucchini
1/3 cup finely chopped raisins
1 1/2 cups self-raising flour

Vanilla Butter Cream
1/2 cup caster sugar
1/3 cup water
125 g unsalted butter
2 teaspoons imitation vanilla
   essence

➤ PREHEAT OVEN to moderate 180°C. Brush a deep, 20 cm baba tin with melted butter or oil.
1 Using electric beaters, beat butter and sugar in small mixing bowl until light and creamy. Add eggs gradually, beating the mixture thoroughly after each addition. Add the essence; beat until just combined.
2 Transfer mixture to large mixing bowl; add zucchini and raisins. Using a metal spoon, fold in sifted flour; stir until just combined and the mixture is almost smooth. Spoon evenly into the prepared tin; smooth surface. Bake for 35 to 40 minutes or until skewer comes out clean when inserted in centre of cake. Leave cake in tin for 10 minutes before turning onto wire rack to cool.
3 To make Vanilla Butter Cream: Combine sugar and water in small pan. Stir constantly over low heat until the mixture boils and sugar has dissolved. Reduce heat, simmer without stirring, uncovered, 5 minutes. Remove from heat; cool. Using electric beaters, beat butter and essence in small mixing bowl until light and creamy.
Pour syrup onto creamed mixture, beating until all has been added and mixture is smooth and fluffy. Spread top and sides of cake with mixture.

COOK'S FILE

Storage time: 3 days in an airtight container in the refrigerator or up to 2 months in the freezer uniced.

BANANA PEANUT BUTTER CAKE

Preparation time: 10 minutes
Cooking time: 1 hour
Makes one 21 cm oblong cake

125 g unsalted butter
½ cup soft brown sugar
¼ cup honey
2 eggs, lightly beaten
⅓ cup crunchy peanut butter
1 cup mashed banana
2 cups wholemeal self-raising
   flour

➤ PREHEAT OVEN to moderate 180°C. Brush a deep, 21 x 14 x 7 cm loaf tin with melted butter or oil. Line the base and sides with paper; grease the paper.

1 Using electric beaters, beat butter, sugar and honey in small mixing bowl until light and creamy. Add eggs gradually, beating thoroughly after each addition. Add peanut butter; beat until combined.

2 Transfer mixture to large mixing bowl; add banana. Using a metal spoon, fold in sifted flour, including husks. Stir until just combined and the mixture is almost smooth.

3 Spoon mixture into prepared tin; smooth surface. Bake 1 hour or until skewer comes out clean when inserted in centre of cake. Leave cake in tin for 10 minutes before turning onto a wire rack to cool. Serve sliced and spread with butter, if desired.

COOK'S FILE

Storage time: Up to 1 week in an airtight container in the refrigerator and 1 month in the freezer.

Hint: Use soft, very ripe bananas for this cake. Mash them with a fork; do not liquidise them in a food processor or they will add too much moisture.

SOUR CREAM PRUNE CAKE

Preparation time: 15 minutes
Cooking time: 35 minutes
Makes one 20 cm baba cake

60 g unsalted butter
60 g cream cheese, softened
⅔ cup caster sugar
1 egg, lightly beaten
2 teaspoons finely grated lemon
   rind
⅓ cup sour cream
½ cup chopped prunes
1⅓ cups self-raising flour

➤ PREHEAT OVEN to moderate
180°C.
1 Brush a deep, 20 cm baba tin with
melted butter or oil.
Using electric beaters, beat butter,
cheese and sugar in small mixing bowl
until light and creamy.
2 Add the egg gradually, beating
thoroughly after each addition. Add
the rind and the sour cream; beat until
just combined.
3 Transfer mixture to a large mixing
bowl; add prunes. Using a metal
spoon, fold in sifted flour. Stir until
mixture is almost smooth.
Pour mixture evenly into prepared tin;
smooth surface. Bake 35 minutes or
until skewer comes out clean when inserted in centre of cake. Leave cake in
tin for 10 minutes before turning onto
a wire rack to cool.

COOK'S FILE

Storage time: 3 days in an airtight
container in the refrigerator or up to
2 months in the freezer.
Hint: Do not overbeat cake mixture
once the sour cream has been added.
Overbeating with electric beaters may
produce a heavy-textured cake.

ZUCCHINI AND APRICOT LOAF

Preparation time: 20 minutes
Cooking time: 50 to 55 minutes
Makes one 25 cm oblong cake

100 g unsalted butter
½ cup caster sugar
2 eggs, lightly beaten
1 teaspoon finely grated lemon rind
1½ cups coarsely grated zucchini
2 tablespoons finely chopped dried apricots
¾ cup wholemeal self-raising flour
½ cup self-raising flour
2 tablespoons milk

Creamy Apricot Topping
⅓ cup finely chopped dried apricots
½ cup water
100 g cream cheese, softened
2 tablespoons icing sugar

➤ PREHEAT OVEN to moderate 180°C. Brush a 25 x 15 x 5.5 cm loaf tin with melted butter or oil. Line base and sides with paper; grease paper.

1 Using electric beaters, beat butter and sugar in small mixing bowl until light and creamy. Add eggs gradually, beating thoroughly after each addition. Add rind, beat until combined.

2 Transfer mixture to large mixing bowl; add zucchini and apricots.
Using a metal spoon, fold in sifted flours, including husks, alternately with milk. Stir until just combined and the mixture is almost smooth. Pour into prepared tin; smooth surface.
Bake 50 to 55 minutes or until skewer comes out clean when inserted in the centre of the cake. Leave cake in tin for

10 minutes before turning onto wire rack to cool.

3 To make the Creamy Apricot Topping: Combine apricots and water in small pan. Stir over high heat until mixture boils. Reduce heat, simmer without stirring, uncovered, for 10 minutes or until almost all liquid is absorbed and the apricots are soft. Remove from heat; cool completely. Using electric beaters, beat cheese and

sifted icing sugar in small mixing bowl until light and creamy. Add the undrained apricot pulp, beating for 2 minutes or until the mixture is almost smooth and is fluffy. Spread sides and top of cake with mixture.

COOK'S FILE

Storage time: 3 days in an airtight container in the refrigerator or up to 2 months in the freezer uniced.

1

2

3

QUICK AND EASY CARROT CAKE

Preparation time: 15 minutes
Cooking time: 45 minutes
Makes one 23 cm square cake

1 cup vegetable oil
3 eggs, lightly beaten
1 cup caster sugar
3 cups coarsely grated carrot
1/3 cup crushed pineapple, well drained
2 tablespoons sultanas

2 teaspoons mixed spice
1¼ cups self-raising flour
1 cup wholemeal self-raising flour

➤ PREHEAT OVEN to moderate 180°C. Brush a deep, 23 cm square cake tin with melted butter or oil. Line the base and sides with paper; grease the paper.

1 Using electric beaters, beat oil, eggs and sugar in small mixing bowl until light and creamy.

2 Transfer mixture to large mixing bowl; add carrot and fruits. Using a metal spoon, fold in the sifted dry ingredients, including husks; stir until just combined.

3 Pour mixture evenly into prepared tin; smooth surface. Bake 45 minutes or until skewer comes out clean when inserted in centre of cake. Leave cake in tin 10 minutes before turning onto wire rack to cool. Serve dusted with sifted icing sugar, if desired.

COOK'S FILE

Storage time: 3 days in an airtight container in the refrigerator or up to 2 months in the freezer.

1

2

3

ORANGE AND SPICE PUMPKIN CAKE

Preparation time: 30 minutes
Cooking time: 45 minutes
Makes one 20 cm round cake

1²⁄₃ cups plain flour
1 teaspoon bicarbonate of soda
½ teaspoon ground nutmeg
½ teaspoon ground ginger
½ teaspoon ground cinnamon
125 g unsalted butter
²⁄₃ cup honey
1 egg, lightly beaten
1 tablespoon finely grated
    orange rind
1 cup/400 g mashed pumpkin,
    well drained
1 cup rolled oats

Orange Cream
125 g cream cheese, softened
½ cup icing sugar
2 teaspoons finely grated
    orange rind
1 tablespoon orange juice

➤ PREHEAT OVEN to moderate 180°C. Brush a deep, 20 cm round cake tin with melted butter or oil. Line base and side with paper; grease paper.
1 Place flour, soda and spices in a food-processor bowl; add butter. Using the pulse action, press the button for 15 seconds or until mixture is a fine crumbly texture.
2 Add honey, egg, rind and pumpkin to bowl, process 10 seconds until the ingredients are just combined. Transfer mixture to a large mixing bowl. Using a metal spoon, fold in the oats.
3 Pour mixture into prepared tin; smooth surface. Bake 45 minutes or until a skewer comes out clean when inserted in centre of cake. Leave cake

in tin 10 minutes before turning onto wire rack to cool.
To make Orange Cream: Using electric beaters, beat cheese and sifted icing sugar in small mixing bowl until light and creamy. Add the rind and juice, beat 3 minutes or until mixture is smooth and fluffy. Spread over top of cake using a flat-bladed knife.

COOK'S FILE

Storage time: 3 days in an airtight container in the refrigerator or up to 2 months in the freezer uniced.

PINEAPPLE COCONUT CAKE

Preparation time: 15 minutes
Cooking time: 45 minutes
Makes one 20 cm baba cake

2 tablespoons desiccated
   coconut
⅔ cup vegetable oil
3 eggs, lightly beaten
⅔ cup caster sugar
2 teaspoons imitation vanilla
   essence
⅔ cup unsweetened crushed
   pineapple, well drained
1 cup desiccated coconut, extra
2 cups self-raising flour
2 tablespoons milk
toasted shredded coconut,
   optional, for decoration

Pineapple Icing
1½ cups icing sugar
2 tablespoons pineapple juice
2 teaspoons unsalted butter

➤ PREHEAT OVEN to moderate 180°C. Brush a deep, 20 cm baba tin with melted butter or oil. Coat base and sides evenly with desiccated coconut; shake off excess.

1 Using electric beaters, beat the oil, eggs, sugar and the essence in a small mixing bowl at high speed for 3 minutes or until mixture is thick and increased in volume.

2 Transfer mixture to large mixing bowl; add pineapple and coconut. Using a metal spoon, fold in the sifted flour alternately with the milk. Stir until just combined and the mixture is almost smooth. Spoon mixture evenly into prepared tin; smooth the surface.

Bake for 45 minutes or until skewer comes out clean when inserted in the centre. Leave the cake in the tin for 5 minutes before turning it onto a wire rack to cool.

3 **To make Pineapple Icing:** Combine sifted icing sugar, juice and butter in a small heatproof bowl. Stand bowl in a pan of simmering water, stirring mixture until the butter has melted and the icing is glossy and smooth. Cool slightly.

Using a spoon, drizzle the icing over the top of the cake, allowing it to run freely down the sides. Scatter the toasted, shredded coconut over the cake, if using.

COOK'S FILE

Storage time: 3 days in an airtight container in the refrigerator or up to 2 months in the freezer uniced.

1

2

3

LAYERED CARAMEL BANANA CAKE

Preparation time: 20 minutes
Cooking time: 45 minutes
Makes one 20 cm round cake

100 g unsalted butter
1/2 cup caster sugar
1 egg, lightly beaten
1 cup mashed banana
2 cups self-raising flour
1/3 cup golden syrup
1/2 teaspoon ground
cinnamon
2/3 cup flaked almonds

➤ PREHEAT OVEN to moderate 180°C.
Brush a round, 20 cm springform tin with melted butter or oil. Line base with paper; grease paper.
1 Using electric beaters, beat butter and sugar in small mixing bowl until light and creamy. Add egg gradually, beating thoroughly after each addition. Transfer the mixture to a large mixing bowl; add banana.
2 Using a metal spoon, fold in sifted flour. Stir until just combined. Reserve 2/3 cup of the mixture.
Spoon the remaining mixture evenly into the prepared tin; smooth surface. Bake for 25 minutes.

3 Combine syrup, cinnamon, almonds and the reserved cake mixture in a small bowl.
Spoon mixture over partly cooked cake; smooth surface. Return the cake to the oven, cook a further 20 minutes or until skewer comes out clean when inserted in centre of cake. Cool cake in tin. Dust with sifted icing sugar to serve, if desired.

COOK'S FILE

Storage time: 2 days in an airtight container in the refrigerator.
Hint: Use a hot spoon for measuring out the golden syrup; this will help it flow freely into the measuring cup.

PINEAPPLE PECAN CAKE

Preparation time: 10 minutes
Cooking time: 35 minutes
Makes one 20 cm round cake

80 g unsalted butter
1/2 cup caster sugar
2 eggs, lightly beaten
1/3 cup finely chopped glacé
pineapple
2 tablespoons finely chopped
pecan nuts
1 cup self-raising flour
2 tablespoons custard powder
2 tablespoons milk

➤ PREHEAT OVEN to moderate 180°C. Brush a deep, 20 cm round cake tin with melted butter or oil. Line base with paper; grease paper.
1 Using electric beaters, beat butter and sugar in small mixing bowl at medium speed until light and creamy. Add eggs, beat for 3 minutes or until just combined.
2 Add pineapple, nuts, sifted flour and custard powder and milk. Beat at low speed 1 minute, until almost smooth.
3 Pour mixture evenly into prepared tin; smooth surface. Bake 35 minutes or until skewer comes out clean when inserted in centre of cake. Leave cake in the tin for 5 minutes before turning

onto a wire rack to cool. Dust with icing sugar before serving, if desired.

COOK'S FILE

Storage time: 3 days in an airtight container in the refrigerator or up to 2 months in the freezer uniced.
Hint: Walnuts and pecans are both rich in oil and similar in texture and are interchangeable in most recipes. Hazelnuts and almonds, which are harder than walnuts and pecans, can also be substituted for each other. Keep stored in an airtight container.
The addition of custard powder will give the cake a pleasing appearance and enrich the flavour.

*Opposite: Layered Caramel Banana Cake (top),
Pineapple Pecan Cake (bottom).*

CARROT CAKE WITH BUTTERSCOTCH FROSTING

Preparation time: 25 minutes
Cooking time: 30 minutes
Makes one shallow 28 cm oblong cake

125 g unsalted butter
½ cup soft brown sugar
2 eggs, lightly beaten
2 teaspoons finely grated
    orange rind
1½ cups finely grated carrot
⅔ cup chopped walnuts
1 teaspoon ground cinnamon
½ teaspoon ground nutmeg
¼ teaspoon ground cloves
1½ cups self-raising flour
1 cup plain flour
¼ cup milk

Butterscotch Frosting
20 g unsalted butter
½ cup soft brown sugar
⅓ cup sour cream
100 g cream cheese, softened

➤ PREHEAT OVEN to moderate 180°C.

1 Brush a shallow, 28 x 18 x 3 cm oblong cake tin with melted butter or oil. Line base and sides with paper; grease the paper.
Using electric beaters, beat butter and sugar in small mixing bowl until light and creamy. Add the eggs gradually, beating thoroughly after each addition. Add rind, beat until combined.

2 Transfer mixture to large mixing bowl. Add carrot and walnuts. Using a metal spoon, fold in sifted spices and flours alternately with the milk. Spoon mixture evenly into the prepared tin;

smooth surface. Bake 30 minutes or until skewer comes out clean when inserted in centre. Leave 10 minutes before turning onto a wire rack to cool.

3 To make Butterscotch Frosting: Combine butter and sugar in a small pan. Stir constantly over low heat until mixture boils and sugar dissolves. Simmer for 3 minutes, uncovered, stirring occasionally. Remove from heat, add sour cream. Stir until combined; cool. Using electric beaters, beat cheese in a small mixing bowl until light and creamy. Add cooled butterscotch mixture gradually, beating thoroughly after each addition. Spread frosting over cake using a flat-bladed knife.

COOK'S FILE

Storage time: 3 days in an airtight container in the refrigerator or up to 2 months in the freezer uniced.

APPLE AND WALNUT CAKE

Preparation time: 15 minutes
Cooking time: 40 minutes
Makes one 20 cm round cake

125 g unsalted butter
1 cup icing sugar
2 eggs, lightly beaten
½ cup chopped walnuts
1⅓ cups plain flour
⅓ cup custard powder
1 teaspoon baking powder
½ teaspoon bicarbonate of soda
2 apples, peeled and cored
2 tablespoons apricot jam
2 teaspoons brandy

➤ PREHEAT OVEN to moderate 180°C.
1 Brush a deep, 20 cm round springform tin with melted butter or oil. Line base with paper; grease paper.
2 Using electric beaters, beat butter and sifted icing sugar in small mixing bowl until creamy and white. Add eggs gradually, beating thoroughly after each addition.
Transfer mixture to a large mixing bowl; add walnuts. Using a metal spoon, fold in sifted dry ingredients. Stir until just combined and mixture is almost smooth.
3 Spoon the mixture evenly into prepared tin; smooth the surface. Cut each apple into quarters, then into thin slices lengthways. Arrange

apples decoratively over top of cake. Bake 40 minutes or until skewer comes out clean when inserted in centre.
4 Combine jam and brandy in small pan. Stir over low heat until mixture boils. Remove from heat, strain into small bowl. Brush warm jam mixture over hot cake. Cool cake in tin.

COOK'S FILE

Storage time: This cake is best eaten on the day it is made.

TEACAKES

BROWNED BUTTER AND CINNAMON TEACAKE

Preparation time: 35 minutes
Cooking time: 40 minutes
Makes one 20 cm square cake

150 g unsalted butter
1½ cups self-raising flour
¼ cup cornflour
1 teaspoon ground cinnamon
¾ cup caster sugar
3 eggs, lightly beaten
1 teaspoon imitation vanilla
    essence
¼ cup orange juice
¼ cup milk

Browned Cinnamon Icing
30 g unsalted butter
50 g unsalted butter, extra
⅓ cup icing sugar
½ teaspoon ground cinnamon
extra ground cinnamon, for
    decoration

➤ PREHEAT OVEN to moderate
180°C. Brush a deep, 20 cm square cake
tin with melted butter or oil, line base
and sides with paper; grease paper.
1 Place the butter in a small pan. Stir
over low heat until melted. Continue to
heat the butter until it turns golden
brown. This process should take about
6 minutes. Skim fat solids from the
surface. Remove from heat.
2 Sift flours and cinnamon into large
mixing bowl. Add the sugar.
Pour the combined eggs, essence, juice,
milk and browned butter onto the dry
ingredients; using electric beaters, beat
on low speed for 3 minutes until just
moistened. Beat mixture on high speed
5 minutes or until it is free of lumps
and increased in volume.
3 Pour mixture into prepared tin;
smooth the surface. Bake 40 minutes
or until skewer comes out clean when
inserted in centre of cake. Leave cake
in tin 10 minutes before turning onto
wire rack to cool.
**To make Browned Cinnamon
Icing:** Brown the 30 g butter as for
Step 1. Using electric beaters, beat
extra butter and sifted icing sugar in
small mixing bowl until light and
creamy. Add cinnamon and browned
butter, beating 2 minutes or until the
mixture is smooth and fluffy. Spread
the icing over the cake using a flat-
bladed knife. Sprinkle with the extra
ground cinnamon.

COOK'S FILE

Storage time: 4 days in an airtight
container or up to 3 months in the
freezer uniced.
Variation: The icing can be made
without browned butter, if preferred.

QUICK AND EASY ORANGE TEACAKE

Preparation time: 10 minutes
Cooking time: 25 minutes
Makes one 20 cm ring cake

1⅓ cups wholemeal self-raising flour
125 g unsalted butter, chopped
1 tablespoon finely grated orange rind
½ cup caster sugar
3 eggs, lightly beaten
2 tablespoons milk

➤ PREHEAT OVEN to moderate 180°C. Brush a 20 cm ring tin with melted butter or oil. Line base with paper; grease paper.

1 Place flour in food-processor bowl; add the butter, rind and sugar. Using the pulse action, press the button for 20 seconds or until mixture is a fine, crumbly texture.

2 Add combined eggs and milk to bowl, process 10 seconds or until mixture is smooth.

3 Spoon mixture into prepared tin; smooth surface. Bake 25 minutes or until skewer comes out clean when inserted in centre of cake.

Leave cake in tin 3 minutes before turning onto wire rack to cool.

COOK'S FILE

Storage time: This cake is best eaten on the day it is made.

Variation: If a food processor is unavailable, this cake can be made successfully with an electric mixer by creaming the butter, rind, sugar and eggs, then folding in the milk and sifted flour (including the husks).

Hint: Be careful when grating the rind of citrus fruits that you do not go too deeply into the skin; the white pith is bitter and should be avoided.

1

2

3

POPPY SEED CAKE WITH LEMON SYRUP

Preparation time: 40 minutes
Cooking time: 25 to 30 minutes
Makes one 20 cm baba cake

1¾ cups self-raising flour
2 tablespoons poppy seeds
185 g unsalted butter
⅔ cup caster sugar
2 tablespoons apricot jam
1 teaspoon finely grated lemon
 rind
¼ cup lemon juice
2 eggs, lightly beaten

Lemon Syrup
½ cup caster sugar
¼ cup lemon juice
½ cup water

➤ PREHEAT OVEN to moderate 180°C. Brush a deep, 20 cm baba tin with melted butter or oil.

1 Sift flour into large mixing bowl. Add the poppy seeds. Make a well in the centre.

Combine butter, sugar, jam, rind and juice in a medium pan. Stir over low heat until butter has melted and sugar has dissolved; remove from heat.

2 Add the butter mixture to the dry ingredients. Using a whisk, stir until just combined; add eggs, mix well; do not overbeat.

Pour mixture into prepared tin; smooth surface. Bake 25 to 30 minutes or until skewer comes out clean when inserted in centre of cake.

3 To make Lemon Syrup: Combine sugar, juice and water in medium pan. Stir constantly over low heat until mixture boils and sugar has dissolved. Reduce heat, simmer without stirring, uncovered, until mixture has thickened and has reduced by one third. Remove from heat, leave 2 minutes for bubbles to subside.

Pour hot syrup over warm cake in tin. Leave until all syrup is absorbed. Turn onto plate. Serve warm with cream.

COOK'S FILE

Storage time: This cake is best eaten the day it is made. Serve warm to fully appreciate the flavour of the syrup.

1

2

3

HONEY AND COCONUT CAKE

Preparation time: 40 minutes
Cooking time: 30 minutes
Makes one 28 cm oblong cake

125 g unsalted butter
⅔ cup raw sugar
2 eggs, lightly beaten
1 teaspoon imitation vanilla
  essence
¼ cup honey
¼ cup desiccated coconut
1¾ cups self-raising flour
1 teaspoon ground nutmeg
¼ teaspoon ground cinnamon
¼ teaspoon ground allspice
½ cup milk
extra ground nutmeg, for
  decoration

Honey and Cream Cheese Icing
125 g cream cheese, softened
½ cup icing sugar
1 tablespoon honey

➤ PREHEAT OVEN to moderate 180°C. Brush a shallow, 28 x 18 x 3 cm oblong cake tin with melted butter or oil, line base and sides with paper; grease paper.

1 Using electric beaters, beat butter and sugar in small mixing bowl until light and creamy. Add eggs gradually, beating thoroughly after each addition. Add essence and honey; beat until combined.

2 Transfer mixture to large mixing bowl; add coconut. Using a metal spoon, fold in sifted flour and spices alternately with milk. Stir until just combined and the mixture is almost smooth. Pour mixture into prepared tin; smooth surface.

3 Bake 30 minutes or until skewer comes out clean when inserted in the

centre of cake. Leave cake in the tin for 10 minutes before turning onto wire rack to cool.

To make Honey and Cream Cheese Icing: Using electric beaters, beat cream cheese in small mixing bowl until creamy. Add sifted icing sugar and the honey, beating 3 minutes or until mix-

ture is smooth and fluffy. Spread the icing over cake using a flat-bladed knife. Sprinkle with extra nutmeg.

COOK'S FILE

Storage time: 4 days in an airtight container or up to 2 months in the freezer uniced.

LEMON BUTTER TEACAKE

Preparation time: 10 minutes
Cooking time: 30 minutes
Makes one 20 cm round cake

50 g unsalted butter
80 g cream cheese, softened
¼ cup honey
**2 tablespoons prepared lemon
    butter**
2 eggs, lightly beaten
1½ cups self-raising flour
¼ cup milk

Lemon Cream Cheese Topping
100 g cream cheese, softened
⅓ cup sour cream
**2 tablespoons prepared lemon
    butter, extra**

➤ PREHEAT OVEN to moderate 180°C. Brush a shallow, 20 cm round cake tin with melted butter or oil. Line base with paper; grease paper.

1 Using electric beaters, beat butter, cream cheese, honey and lemon butter in small mixing bowl at medium speed until light and creamy. Add eggs, beat 1 minute or until just combined.

2 Add flour and milk, beat at low speed 1 minute or until mixture is smooth. Pour mixture evenly into prepared tin; smooth surface. Bake for 30 minutes or until skewer comes out clean when inserted in centre of cake.

3 Leave cake in tin 5 minutes before turning onto wire rack to cool.

To make Lemon Cream Cheese Topping: Beat cream cheese, sour cream and lemon butter in small mixing bowl until light and creamy. Spread over cake using flat-bladed knife.

COOK'S FILE

Storage time: This cake is best eaten on the day it is made.

APPLE AND CINNAMON TEACAKE

Preparation time: 15 minutes
Cooking time: 30 minutes
Makes one 20 cm round cake

60 g unsalted butter
⅓ cup caster sugar
½ teaspoon ground cinnamon
1 egg, lightly beaten
½ cup pie apple, chopped
1¼ cups self-raising flour
¼ cup milk

Cinnamon Icing
1 tablespoon water
15 g unsalted butter
¼ cup caster sugar
½ teaspoon ground cinnamon

➤ PREHEAT OVEN to moderate 180°C. Brush a 20 cm round springform tin with melted butter or oil. Line base and side with paper; grease paper.

1 Using electric beaters, beat butter, sugar and cinnamon in small mixing bowl at medium speed until light and creamy. Add egg, beat 1 minute or until just combined.

2 Add the apple, sifted flour and milk. Beat at low speed for 1 minute or until mixture is almost smooth.
Pour mixture evenly into prepared tin; smooth surface. Bake 30 minutes or until skewer comes out clean when inserted in centre of cake.

3 Leave cake in tin 10 minutes before turning onto wire rack to cool.

To make Cinnamon Icing: Combine all the ingredients in a small pan.
Stir constantly over low heat until mixture boils and sugar has dissolved. Simmer without stirring, uncovered, for 2 minutes. Using a flat-bladed knife, spread the warm icing over the top of the warm cake.

COOK'S FILE

Storage time: This cake is best eaten on the day it is made.

Variation: Substitute ground mixed spice for cinnamon in cake and icing. This cake can be served as a dessert with whipped cream.

CARDAMOM APPLE CAKE

Preparation time: 30 minutes
Cooking time: 55 minutes
Makes one 20 cm round cake

2 green apples, peeled, cored
¼ cup soft brown sugar
150 g unsalted butter
¾ cup caster sugar
2 eggs, lightly beaten
1 teaspoon imitation vanilla
   essence
2 cups self-raising flour
2 teaspoons ground cardamom
½ cup milk

➤ PREHEAT OVEN to moderate 180°C. Brush a deep, 20 cm round cake tin with melted butter or oil, line base and side with paper; grease paper.

1 Slice one apple in thin rings and finely chop the other one. Place rings of apple in the base of cake tin, overlapping each piece. Sprinkle with brown sugar.

2 Using electric beaters, beat butter and sugar in small mixing bowl until light and creamy. Add eggs gradually, beating thoroughly after each addition. Add essence; beat until combined. Transfer mixture to large mixing bowl; add chopped apple.

3 Using a metal spoon, fold in the sifted flour and the cardamom alternately with the milk. Stir until just combined and the mixture is almost smooth.

Spoon mixture into prepared tin; smooth surface. Bake 55 minutes or until skewer comes out clean when inserted in centre of cake.

Leave cake in tin 20 minutes before turning onto wire rack to cool.

COOK'S FILE

Storage time: This cake is best eaten the day it is made.

Variation: Decorate the top of the cake with strips of glacé or crystallised fruit or ginger, if desired.

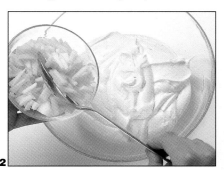

TREACLE GINGER LOAF

Preparation time: 25 minutes
Cooking time: 40 minutes
Makes one 21 cm oblong cake

100 g unsalted butter
½ cup caster sugar
¼ cup soft dark brown sugar
2 eggs, lightly beaten
¼ cup black treacle
⅔ cup self-raising flour
½ cup plain flour
1 tablespoon ground ginger
¼ cup milk
icing sugar, for decoration

➤ PREHEAT OVEN to moderate 180°C. Brush a deep, 21 x 14 x 7 cm loaf tin with melted butter or oil, line base and sides with paper; grease paper.

1 Using electric beaters, beat butter and sugars in small mixing bowl until light and creamy. Add eggs gradually, beating thoroughly after each addition. Add treacle; beat until combined.

2 Transfer mixture to large mixing bowl. Using a metal spoon, fold in the sifted flours and ginger alternately with the milk.

3 Pour mixture into prepared tin; smooth surface.

Bake 40 minutes or until skewer comes out clean when inserted in centre of cake. Leave cake in tin 20 minutes before turning onto wire rack to cool. Dust cake with sifted icing sugar.

COOK'S FILE

Storage time: 1 week in an airtight container or up to 3 months in the freezer.

Variation: Use golden syrup instead of treacle. Treacle has a richer flavour; it is a molasses-like sugar syrup used in toffees and old-fashioned desserts.

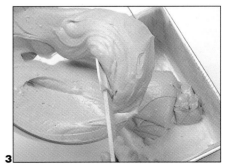

CHERRY TEACAKE

Preparation time: 15 minutes
Cooking time: 30 minutes
Makes one 20 cm round cake

60 g unsalted butter
⅔ cup caster sugar
½ teaspoon coconut essence
3 eggs, lightly beaten
⅓ cup chopped glacé cherries
¼ cup desiccated coconut
1¼ cups self-raising flour
⅓ cup cornflour

Pink Icing
½ cup icing sugar

1 teaspoon unsalted butter
2 teaspoons boiling water
pink food colouring

➤ PREHEAT OVEN to moderate 180°C.
1 Brush a deep, 20 cm round cake tin with melted butter or oil. Line base with paper; grease paper.
Using electric beaters, beat butter, sugar and essence in small mixing bowl at medium speed until light and creamy.
2 Add eggs, beat 3 minutes or until just combined. Transfer the mixture to a large mixing bowl. Add cherries and coconut and sifted flour and cornflour, beat at low speed for 1 minute or until

mixture is almost smooth. Spoon mixture evenly into prepared tin; smooth surface. Bake 30 minutes or until skewer comes out clean when inserted in centre. Leave cake in tin 10 minutes before turning onto wire rack to cool.
3 To make Pink Icing: Combine sifted icing sugar, butter and water in a small bowl to form a firm paste. Stand bowl in pan of simmering water, stir until icing is smooth and glossy; remove from heat. Tint icing with colouring as desired. Spread icing over top of cake using a flat-bladed knife.

COOK'S FILE

Storage time: This cake is best eaten on the day it is made.

DATE AND WALNUT LOAF

Preparation time: 25 minutes
Cooking time: 1 hour
Makes one 21 cm oblong cake

125 g unsalted butter
½ cup honey
¼ cup soft brown sugar
2 tablespoons milk
1½ cups finely chopped dates
1 teaspoon bicarbonate of soda
2 cups plain flour
½ teaspoon ground nutmeg
1 cup chopped walnuts
2 eggs, lightly beaten

➤ PREHEAT OVEN to moderate 180°C.
1 Brush a deep, 21 x 14 x 7 cm loaf tin with melted butter or oil.
Line base and two sides of tin with paper; grease paper.
2 Combine butter, honey, sugar and milk in a medium pan. Stir over low heat until butter has melted and sugar has dissolved; remove from heat.
Add dates and soda; stir, set aside to cool. Sift flour with nutmeg into large mixing bowl. Add the walnuts. Make a well in the centre.
3 Add butter mixture and eggs to dry ingredients. Using a wooden spoon, stir until well combined; do not overbeat.

Pour mixture evenly into prepared tin; smooth surface. Bake 1 hour or until skewer comes out clean when inserted in centre of cake.
Leave loaf in tin 10 minutes before turning onto wire rack to cool. Serve loaf with butter if desired.

COOK'S FILE

Storage time: This cake is best eaten on the day it is made.
Hint: Honey is useful for its flavour and keeping properties. Cakes made with honey stay moist longer than those made with sugar. The flavour of the honey is determined by the kind of flower the bees have visited.

1

2

3

VANILLA CURRANT TWIST

Preparation time: 15 minutes
Cooking time: 40 minutes
Makes one 26 cm bar cake

1 cup self-raising flour
½ cup plain flour
30 g unsalted butter, chopped
¼ cup caster sugar
¼ cup currants
1 egg
2 tablespoons milk
1½ teaspoons vanilla essence
1 teaspoon milk, extra
icing sugar, for decoration

➤ PREHEAT OVEN to moderate 180°C.

1 Brush a 26 x 8 x 4.5 cm bar tin with melted butter or oil. Line base and two sides with paper; grease paper.

Sift flours into large mixing bowl; add chopped butter and sugar.

Using fingertips, rub butter into flour for 2 minutes or until the mixture is a fine, crumbly texture.

2 Add currants; stir. Add combined egg, milk and essence to bowl, stir to form a soft, sticky dough.

Turn the mixture onto a lightly floured surface, knead quickly 1 minute or until smooth.

3 Form dough into a 50-cm long log. Fold log in half and twist.

Place twist in prepared tin; brush the surface with the extra milk. Bake for 40 minutes or until skewer comes out clean when inserted in centre. Invert twist onto wire rack to cool.

Dust the twist with sifted icing sugar just before serving.

COOK'S FILE

Storage time: This cake is best eaten on the day it is made.

1

2

3

TRADITIONAL FRUIT CAKES

WHOLEMEAL FRUIT AND NUT CAKE

Preparation time: 45 minutes
Cooking time: 2 hours 30 minutes
to 3 hours
Makes one 20 cm square cake

180 g unsalted butter
3/4 cup soft dark brown sugar
3 eggs, lightly beaten
200 g figs, chopped
1 cup/200 g dried apricots,
chopped
2/3 cup/100 g currants
1/2 cup/100 g sultanas
1 cup/100 g walnut pieces
1/2 cup sunflower kernels
1 1/2 cups plain wholemeal flour
1/2 cup self-raising flour
1 teaspoon ground cinnamon
1 teaspoon ground nutmeg
1 teaspoon ground allspice
1/2 cup apricot nectar

Spicy Nut Topping
1/4 cup finely chopped walnuts
1 tablespoon sunflower kernels
1/2 teaspoon ground cinnamon
1/2 teaspoon ground nutmeg
1/2 teaspoon ground allspice

➤ PREHEAT OVEN to moderately slow 160°C.
1 Brush a deep, 20 cm square cake tin with melted butter or oil. Line base and sides with paper; grease paper.
Using electric beaters, beat butter and sugar in small mixing bowl until light and creamy. Add the eggs gradually, beating thoroughly after each addition.
2 Transfer mixture to large mixing bowl; add fruit, walnuts and kernels. Using a metal spoon, fold in the sifted dry ingredients alternately with the apricot nectar. Stir until the mixture is almost smooth.
3 Spoon mixture evenly into prepared tin; smooth the surface.
To make the Spicy Nut Topping: Combine all the topping ingredients. Spoon mixture onto the top of the cake, pressing it down firmly with the back of the spoon.
Bake 2 1/2 to 3 hours or until skewer comes out clean when inserted in centre of cake. Leave cake in the tin for 3 to 4 hours before turning out.

COOK'S FILE

Storage time: Because this cake does not contain alcohol, it should be eaten within 4 weeks of baking. Store in an airtight container.

BEST EVER RICH FRUIT CAKE

Preparation time: 45 minutes
Cooking time: 3 to 3 hours
   30 minutes
Makes one 20 cm round cake

250 g unsalted butter
1 cup soft dark brown sugar
5 eggs, lightly beaten
1 tablespoon coffee
   essence
1 teaspoon imitation vanilla
   essence
1 tablespoon molasses
1 tablespoon plum jam
¼ cup orange juice
2 teaspoons finely grated
   orange rind
1¼ cups/250 g sultanas
1¼ cups/250 g currants
1¼ cups/250 g raisins
⅔ cup/125 g chopped peel
½ cup/125 g glacé cherries, cut
   in halves
½ cup/100 g glacé apricots,
   chopped
½ cup/100 g glacé pineapple,
   chopped
½ cup/100 g figs, chopped
⅔ cup/80 g slivered almonds
2 cups plain flour
½ cup self-raising flour
2 teaspoons mixed spice
½ cup sherry, brandy or rum
¼ cup warmed, sieved
   apricot jam

Fondant Icing
1 kg pure icing sugar
5 teaspoons gelatine
¼ cup water
½ cup liquid glucose
1 tablespoon glycerine
1 cup pure icing sugar,
   extra, for kneading

Decorations
1 metre ribbon or lace
1 small posy of fresh flowers

➤ PREHEAT OVEN to slow 150°C. Line base and side of a deep, 20 cm round cake tin with greaseproof paper.

1 Using electric beaters, beat butter and sugar in small mixing bowl until light and creamy. Add eggs gradually, beating thoroughly after each addition. Add essences, molasses, plum jam, juice and rind; beat until combined.

2 Transfer mixture to large mixing bowl; add fruit and almonds. Using metal spoon, fold in the sifted dry ingredients alternately with sherry. Stir until just combined and the mixture is almost smooth.

3 Spoon mixture evenly into prepared tin; sprinkle top with cold water and smooth surface with a wetted hand. Tap cake tin gently on bench top to settle mixture.

Wrap double thickness of brown paper around tin, secure with paper clip. Bake for 3 to 3½ hours or until skewer comes out clean when inserted in centre of cake. Leave cake in tin overnight before turning out.

4 To make Fondant Icing: Sift icing sugar into large mixing bowl. In small pan, dissolve gelatine in cold water. Add glucose, place over gentle heat, stirring occasionally until the gelatine has dissolved. Remove from heat, stir in glycerine. Cool 1 minute. Make a well in centre of icing sugar and pour in the gelatine mixture. Use wooden spoon to thoroughly combine. Knead by hand until mixture is a firm, dough-like paste.

Turn mixture onto a smooth surface lightly covered with sifted icing sugar. Knead well until smooth and pliable; mixture should resemble Plasticine. Cover fondant securely with plastic wrap until needed. Do not refrigerate.

Best used within 2 days of making.

5 To cover cake with fondant, place cake upside down on a covered cake board or large, flat plate. Brush cake lightly and evenly with sieved jam. Knead fondant with the extra sifted icing sugar until smooth. Roll out evenly on a smooth surface lightly covered with icing sugar until 1 cm thick; try to roll out in the shape of the cake. Move icing constantly to prevent it sticking to the work surface.

Lift onto cake using rolling pin. Roll

rolling pin gently onto top of cake. Ease the icing around sides and base of cake.

Coat the palms of your hands lightly with icing sugar and rub top and sides of cake lightly for 2 to 3 minutes until icing is smooth. Cut away excess from base using sharp knife.

Cake is best left for 2 days in a clean, cool place before decorating. Do not refrigerate.

6 Soften a small amount of icing to a paste with a little hot water. Wrap ribbon or lace around cake, secure with a little of the softened icing.

Hold in place with a pin until icing dries. Trim excess ribbon using small, sharp scissors. Tie a bow from remaining ribbon, place over ribbon join, using icing paste on back to secure. Place posy of small flowers on top of cake just prior to serving.

COOK'S FILE

Storage time: Uniced cake can be kept for up to 3 months. Store, covered in several layers of plastic wrap, in the refrigerator. Iced cake will keep for up to 3 months at room temperature. Keep in a cool, dark, dust-free place. Iced cake can also be frozen for up to 12 months. Store in freezer in a rigid plastic container.

Variation: Cake may be covered with 750 g purchased marzipan before adding fondant icing. Follow same instructions for fondant icing. Leave marzipan to dry for at least 24 hours before applying fondant.

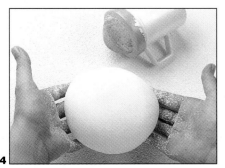

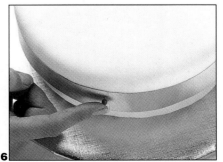

CLASSIC BOILED FRUIT CAKE

Preparation time: 30 minutes
Cooking time: 1 to 1 hour 15 minutes
Makes one 20 cm round cake

1¼ cups self-raising flour
1¼ cups plain flour
250 g unsalted butter
1 cup soft dark brown sugar
2 cups/375 g mixed dried fruit
1⅓ cups/200 g pitted prunes,
  chopped
1¼ cups port
½ teaspoon bicarbonate of soda
2 eggs, lightly beaten

➤ PREHEAT OVEN to moderate 180°C. Line the base and side of a deep, 20 cm round cake tin with greaseproof paper. Sift flours into large mixing bowl.

1 Combine butter, sugar, dried fruit, prunes and port in medium pan.
Stir over low heat until butter has melted and sugar has dissolved. Bring to the boil and simmer, uncovered, for 5 minutes.

2 Remove from heat, stir in soda and set aside to cool. Add eggs, mix well. Pour the mixture onto the sifted flours, mix well.

3 Pour mixture evenly into prepared tin; smooth the surface. Bake cake for 1 to 1¼ hours or until skewer comes out clean when inserted in centre of cake. Leave cake in tin 1 hour before turning out.

COOK'S FILE

Storage time: Store, covered with several layers of plastic wrap, for up to 2 months in the refrigerator.
Variation: Packeted mixed dried fruit was used; substitute any combination of your favourite dried fruits.

AMERICAN-STYLE FESTIVE FRUIT CAKE

Preparation time: 30 minutes
Cooking time: 1 to 1 hour 15 minutes
Makes two bar tin cakes

125 g unsalted butter
¼ cup soft brown sugar
2 eggs, lightly beaten
¼ cup golden syrup
250 g dates, pitted
125 g glacé pineapple, cut into
    2 cm pieces
125 g glacé apricots, cut into
    2 cm pieces
200 g whole red glacé cherries
125 g whole macadamia nuts
125 g whole brazil nuts
125 g whole hazelnuts
¼ cup self-raising flour
¼ cup plain flour
2 tablespoons port or brandy

➤ PREHEAT OVEN to slow 150°C.
Line the bases and the sides of two
26 x 8 x 4.5 cm bar tins with greaseproof paper.
1 Using electric beaters, beat butter
and sugar in small mixing bowl until
light and creamy. Add eggs gradually,
beating thoroughly after each addition.
Add syrup; beat until combined.
2 Transfer mixture to large mixing
bowl; add fruit and nuts. Using a
metal spoon, fold in the sifted ingredients alternately with the liquid.
Stir until just combined and mixture is
almost smooth.
3 Spoon mixture evenly into prepared
tins; smooth surface. Bake 1¼ hours
or until skewer comes out clean when
inserted in centre of cakes. Leave
cakes in tins 1 hour before turning out.

COOK'S FILE

Storage time: Cake will keep in an
airtight container in the refrigerator
for up to 3 months.
Hint: Best served in thin slices. Cake
can be baked in a ring tin, if desired.
Decorate with Christmas ribbon and
use as centrepiece for your table.

GREAT VALUE FRUIT CAKE

Preparation time: 1 hour
Cooking time: 3 to 3 hours 30 minutes
Makes one 20 cm square cake

250 g unsalted butter
1 cup soft brown sugar
4 eggs, lightly beaten
1 teaspoon imitation vanilla
   essence
1 tablespoons orange marmalade
1 tablespoon golden syrup
1.25 kg mixed dried fruit
2 cups plain flour
1/2 cup self-raising flour
2 teaspoons mixed spice
1 teaspoon ground cinnamon
1/2 cup rum, brandy or port

Royal Icing
4 egg whites
5 1/2 cups pure sifted icing sugar
2 teaspoons lemon juice

Decorations
1 metre red, green or tartan
   ribbon
selection of small Christmas
ornaments

➤ PREHEAT OVEN to slow 150°C. Line the base and the sides of a deep, 20 cm square cake tin with grease-proof paper.

1 Using electric beaters, beat butter and sugar in small mixing bowl until light and creamy. Add eggs gradually, beating thoroughly after each addition. Add essence, marmalade and golden syrup; beat until combined.

2 Transfer mixture to a large mixing bowl; add fruit. Using a metal spoon, fold in the sifted dry ingredients alternately with liquid. Stir until just combined and mixture is almost smooth.

Spoon mixture evenly into prepared tin; sprinkle top with cold water and smooth surface with wetted hand.

3 Tap cake tin gently on bench top to settle mixture. Wrap double thickness of brown paper around cake tin; secure with a paper clip. Bake cake for 3 to 3 1/2 hours or until skewer comes out clean when inserted in centre. Leave cake overnight before turning out.

4 To make Royal Icing: Using electric beaters, beat egg whites in a clean, dry mixing bowl for 30 seconds. Add icing sugar, 1 tablespoon at a time, beating continuously on a slow speed until mixture is very stiff and stands in peaks. Blend in lemon juice. Cover with damp cloth or plastic wrap to prevent icing drying out.

5 Place cake on large plate or cake board. Using a flat-bladed knife, cover cake completely with icing, reserving 2 tablespoons for decoration. Use the knife to work icing into fluffy peaks all over the cake. Leave cake for 2 hours to allow icing to harden.

6 Wrap ribbon around cake, secure with small amount of Royal Icing. Trim excess ribbon, tie into a bow, trim edges. Place a small amount of Royal Icing on back of bow, place bow over ribbon join, secure with a pin; remove pin when icing is firm. Position ornaments on cake, securing them with a small amount of icing.

COOK'S FILE

Storage time: Uniced cake can be kept for up to 3 months. Store, covered with several layers of plastic wrap, in the refrigerator. Iced cake will keep for up to 2 weeks at room temperature.

Hint: Royal Icing sets very quickly so it is important to work fast when icing the cake.

The icing may be coloured with food colourings from supermarkets or cake-decorating speciality shops.

1

2

3

4

5

6

CURRANT CAKE

Preparation time: 25 minutes
Cooking time: 2 hours 30 minutes
to 3 hours
Makes one 20 cm round cake

250 g unsalted butter
1 cup soft brown sugar
4 eggs, lightly beaten
2 tablespoons lime marmalade
1 kg currants
2 cups plain flour
1 teaspoon mixed spice
¾ cup whisky

➤ PREHEAT OVEN to moderately slow 160°C. Line base and side of a deep, 20 cm round cake tin with greaseproof paper.

1 Using electric beaters, beat butter and sugar in small mixing bowl until light and creamy. Add eggs gradually, beating thoroughly after each addition. Add marmalade; beat until combined.

2 Transfer mixture to large mixing bowl; add fruit. Using a metal spoon, fold in sifted ingredients alternately with whisky. Stir until just combined and mixture is almost smooth.

3 Spoon the mixture evenly into the prepared tin; smooth the surface. Bake for 2½ to 3 hours or until a skewer comes out clean when inserted in centre of cake. Leave cake in tin for several hours or overnight to cool.

COOK'S FILE

Storage time: Up to 2 months. Store, covered with several layers of plastic wrap, in the refrigerator.

Variation: Any flavour and texture of marmalade can be used.

Hint: The currants can be soaked overnight in half the measured amount of whisky (or brandy, if preferred). This will give a slightly moister cake.

BOILED GINGER FRUIT CAKE

Preparation time: 30 minutes
Cooking time: 1 to 1 hour 15 minutes
Makes one 20 cm square cake

1¼ cups self-raising flour
1¼ cups plain flour
250 g unsalted butter
1 cup soft dark brown sugar
1 cup/200 g dates, chopped
1 cup/200 g raisins
1 cup/200 g sultanas
½ cup/100 g chopped glacé ginger
⅔ cup green ginger wine

⅓ cup apple juice
2 teaspoons ground ginger
½ teaspoon bicarbonate of soda
2 eggs, lightly beaten

➤ PREHEAT OVEN to moderate 180°C. Line the base and the sides of a deep, 20 cm square cake tin with greaseproof paper.

1 Sift flours into large mixing bowl. Combine butter, sugar, fruits, ginger wine, juice and ground ginger in a medium pan. Stir over low heat until the butter has melted and the sugar has dissolved; bring to the boil and simmer, uncovered, for 5 minutes.

2 Remove from heat, stir in soda, set aside to cool. Add eggs and mix well.

Add fruit mixture to flours, stir with a metal spoon until just combined; do not overbeat.

3 Pour mixture evenly into prepared tin; smooth surface.

Bake for 1 to 1¼ hours or until skewer comes out clean when inserted in centre of cake. Leave cake in the tin for 1 hour before turning out.

COOK'S FILE

Storage time: Up to 2 months. Store, covered with several layers of plastic wrap, in the refrigerator.

Variation: To add extra flavour and moistness, pour 2 tablespoons of green ginger wine over cake when it is still hot from the oven.

Opposite: Currant Cake (top),
Boiled Ginger Fruit Cake (bottom).

DUNDEE CAKE

Preparation time: 30 minutes
Cooking time: 2 to 2 hours
    30 minutes
Makes one 20 cm round cake

250 g unsalted butter
1 cup soft brown sugar
4 eggs, lightly beaten
1 cup/200 g raisins
1 cup/200 g sultanas
1⅓ cups/200 g currants
⅓ cup/60 g combined orange
    and lemon peel
¼ cup/60 g glacé cherries,
    chopped

1 cup/100 g almond meal
¾ cup/100 g slivered almonds
1½ cups plain flour
½ cup self-raising flour
2 tablespoons rum
100 g whole almonds, for
    decoration

➤ PREHEAT OVEN to slow 150˚C.
1 Brush a deep, 20 cm round cake tin with melted butter or oil. Line base and side with greaseproof paper. Using electric beaters, beat butter and sugar in small mixing bowl until light and creamy. Add the eggs gradually, beating thoroughly after each addition.
2 Transfer mixture to large mixing bowl; add fruits, peel and nuts. Using a metal spoon, fold in the sifted dry ingredients alternately with liquid. Stir until just combined and the mixture is almost smooth.
3 Spoon mixture evenly into the tin; smooth surface. Arrange almonds on top of cake. Bake for 2 to 2½ hours or until skewer comes out clean when inserted in centre of cake. Leave cake in tin several hours before turning out.

COOK'S FILE

Storage time: Up to 2 months. Store, covered with several layers of plastic wrap, in the refrigerator.
Hint: All traditional fruit cakes must be left to cool in tin for the specified time. If turned out hot, they will break.

1

2

3

LIGHT FRUIT CAKE

Preparation time: 35 minutes
Cooking time: 3 to 3 hours 30 minutes
Makes one 20 cm round cake

250 g unsalted butter
1 cup caster sugar
4 eggs, lightly beaten
1 teaspoon imitation vanilla
  essence
1 kg mixed dried fruit
1½ cups plain flour
½ cup self-raising flour
½ cup sherry
125 g assorted glacé fruits
60 g walnut halves

➤ PREHEAT OVEN to moderately slow 160°C. Line base and side of a deep, 20 cm round cake tin with greaseproof paper.

1 Using electric beaters, beat butter and sugar in small mixing bowl until light and creamy. Add eggs gradually, beating thoroughly after each addition. Add essence; beat until combined.

2 Transfer mixture to large mixing bowl; add dried fruit. Using a metal spoon, fold in sifted dry ingredients alternately with the sherry. Stir until just combined and mixture is almost smooth.

3 Spoon mixture evenly into prepared tin; smooth surface. Decorate top with glacé fruits and walnuts. Bake for 3 to 3½ hours or until skewer comes out clean when inserted in centre of cake. Leave cake in tin for several hours or overnight to cool.

COOK'S FILE

Storage time: Up to 1 month. Store, covered with several layers of plastic wrap, in the refrigerator.

Variation: Packeted mixed dried fruit has been used for this recipe but any combination of dried and glacé fruits to the same weight can be used. The alcohol and nuts used can also be varied, depending on your taste.
The glacé fruits and walnuts could be omitted for decoration and the cake iced, if preferred.

TWELFTH NIGHT CAKE

Preparation time: 45 minutes
Cooking time: 3 to 3 hours 30 minutes
Makes one 20 cm round cake

250 g unsalted butter
1 cup caster sugar
4 eggs, lightly beaten
2 teaspoons finely grated lemon
   rind
3½ cups/500 g currants
1 cup/155 g mixed peel
½ cup/60 g almonds, chopped
2 cups plain flour
½ cup self-raising flour
½ cup brandy
100 g glacé or crystallised
   orange and lemon slices, for
   decoration

Lemon Glaze
⅓ cup lemon juice
¼ cup icing sugar

➤ PREHEAT OVEN to moderately
slow 160°C. Line the base and side of
a deep, 20 cm round cake tin with
greaseproof paper.

1 Using electric beaters, beat butter
and sugar in small mixing bowl until
light and creamy.
Add the eggs gradually, beating
thoroughly after each addition. Add
rind; beat until combined. Transfer the
mixture to a large mixing bowl; add
fruit and almonds.

2 Using a metal spoon, fold in sifted
flours alternately with the brandy. Stir
until just combined and the mixture is
almost smooth. Spoon mixture evenly
into prepared tin; smooth surface.

Bake cake for 3 to 3½ hours or until
skewer comes out clean when inserted
in centre of cake. Leave cake in tin for
20 minutes before turning onto wire
rack. Do not remove lining paper.

3 To make the Lemon Glaze:
Combine the lemon juice and sifted
icing sugar, stir until well mixed. Pour
the mixture over the warm cake. Leave
to set for 5 minutes. Remove the lining
paper and decorate the top of the cake
with the orange and lemon slices.

COOK'S FILE

Storage time: Make up to 2 weeks
ahead. Store, covered with plastic
wrap, in the refrigerator.
Hint: Icing sugar is commercially
made by milling granulated sugar to a
fine powder. You can't achieve the
same effect by using a food-processor.

1

2

3

WHISKY AND SPICE FRUIT CAKE

Preparation time: 45 minutes
Cooking time: 1 to 1 hour 15 minutes
Makes one 20 cm square cake

250 g unsalted butter
½ cup caster sugar
½ cup soft dark brown sugar
4 eggs, separated
3 cups/500 g raisins
1½ cups plain flour
1 cup self-raising flour
2 teaspoons mixed spice
1 teaspoon ground cinnamon
1 teaspoon ground cardamom
1 teaspoon ground cloves
¾ cup Scotch whisky

Honey Frosting
90 g cream cheese, softened
2 teaspoons honey
1 teaspoon finely grated lemon
    rind
1½ cups icing sugar

➤ PREHEAT OVEN to moderately slow 160°C. Brush a deep, 20 cm square cake tin with melted butter or oil. Line base and sides with paper; grease paper.

1 Using electric beaters, beat butter and sugars in small mixing bowl until light and creamy. Add the egg yolks gradually, beating thoroughly after each addition.

2 Transfer the mixture to a large mixing bowl; add the raisins. Using a metal spoon, fold in sifted dry ingredients alternately with whisky. Stir until just combined and the mixture is almost smooth.

3 Using electric beaters, beat egg whites in small mixing bowl until soft peaks form. Using a metal spoon, fold through cake mixture.

Spoon mixture evenly into prepared tin; smooth the surface. Bake for 1 to 1¼ hours or until skewer comes out clean when inserted in centre of cake. Leave cake in tin 20 minutes before turning onto wire rack to cool.

To make Honey Frosting: Beat cream cheese, honey and rind in small mixing bowl until light and creamy.

Add sifted icing sugar, beating for 3 to 4 minutes or until mixture is smooth and fluffy. Spread on top of cake.

COOK'S FILE

Storage time: Cake is best eaten within 1 week of making. Uniced cake can be kept for up to 3 weeks. Store in an airtight container.

CELEBRATION CAKES

PASSIONFRUIT TORTE

Preparation time: 15 minutes
Cooking time: 50 minutes
Makes one 23 cm round cake

200 g unsalted butter
1 cup caster sugar
3 eggs, lightly beaten
¼ cup fresh passionfruit pulp
2½ cups self-raising flour
⅔ cup milk
1¼ cups cream

Passionfruit Cream
½ cup caster sugar
¼ cup fresh passionfruit pulp
2 egg whites

➤ PREHEAT OVEN to moderate 180°C. Brush a deep, 23 cm round cake tin with melted butter or oil. Line base and side with paper; grease paper.
Using electric beaters, beat butter and sugar in a small mixing bowl until light and creamy. Add the eggs gradually, beating thoroughly after each addition. Add passionfruit pulp; beat until combined.
1 Transfer mixture to large mixing bowl. Using a metal spoon, fold in sifted flour alternately with milk. Stir until just combined and mixture is smooth.
Spoon mixture evenly into prepared tin; smooth surface. Bake 50 minutes or until skewer comes out clean when inserted in centre of cake. Leave cake in tin 15 minutes before turning onto wire rack to cool.
2 To make Passionfruit Cream: Combine sugar and passionfruit pulp in small pan. Stir constantly over low heat until mixture boils and sugar has dissolved. Simmer without stirring, uncovered, 3 minutes; remove from heat. Using electric beaters, beat egg whites in a clean, dry mixing bowl until stiff peaks form.
Pour hot passionfruit mixture in thin stream over egg whites, beating constantly until cream is thick, glossy and increased in volume.
3 Turn cake upside down. Cut horizontally into four layers. Divide the Passionfruit Cream into three even portions. Place first layer on a serving plate. Spread the cake evenly with the Passionfruit Cream.
Continue layering with remaining cake and Passionfruit Cream, ending with cake. Using electric beaters, beat cream in a small mixing bowl until stiff peaks form. Using a flat-bladed knife, spread the cream over top and side of cake.

COOK'S FILE

Storage time: This is best assembled and eaten the day it is made. It can be decorated up to 3 hours before serving. Store, uncovered, in the refrigerator.

BLACK FOREST CAKE

Preparation time: 1 hour 15 minutes
Cooking time: 40 to 50 minutes
Makes one 23 cm round cake

200 g unsalted butter
¾ cup caster sugar
3 eggs, lightly beaten
1 teaspoon imitation vanilla
     essence
1⅔ cups self-raising flour
⅓ cup plain flour
¾ cup cocoa powder
1 tablespoon instant coffee
     powder
½ teaspoon bicarbonate
     of soda
½ cup buttermilk
⅓ cup milk
1¼ cups cream, whipped
425 g can pitted cherries,
     drained

white and dark chocolate curls,
     for decoration (see page 11)

Chocolate Mock Cream
**200 g dark chocolate, chopped
250 g unsalted butter**

➤ PREHEAT OVEN to moderate
180°C. Brush a deep, 23 cm round cake
tin with melted butter or oil, line base
and side with paper; grease paper.
1 Using electric beaters, beat butter
and sugar in small mixing bowl until
light and creamy. Add eggs gradually,
beating thoroughly after each addition.
Add essence; beat until combined.
2 Transfer mixture to large mixing
bowl. Using a metal spoon, fold in
sifted flours, cocoa, coffee and soda
alternately with combined buttermilk
and milk. Stir until just combined and
the mixture is almost smooth.
3 Pour mixture evenly into prepared
tin; smooth the surface. Bake for 40 to

50 minutes or until skewer comes out
clean when inserted in centre of cake.
Leave cake in tin 20 minutes before
turning onto wire rack to cool.
**4 To make Chocolate Mock
Cream:** Place chocolate in glass bowl.
Stir over barely simmering water until

melted; remove from heat. Beat butter in small mixing bowl until light and creamy. Add chocolate, beating 1 minute or until mixture is glossy and smooth.

5 Turn cake upside down. Cut into three layers horizontally. Place first layer on serving plate. Spread cake evenly with half the whipped cream, top with half the cherries. Continue layering with remaining cake, cream and cherries, ending with cake on top.

6 Spread Mock Cream over top and sides, using a flat-bladed knife. Using a piping bag, pipe stars of remaining mixture around cake rim. Decorate top with chocolate curls (refer to page 11).

COOK'S FILE

Storage time: This cake and its filling is best assembled and eaten on the day that it is made.

ITALIAN LIQUEUR CAKE

Preparation time: 1 hour 30 minutes
Cooking time: 50 minutes
Makes one 20 cm round cake

1 cup self-raising flour
1 tablespoon cornflour
2 tablespoons rice flour
5 eggs, lightly beaten
¾ cup caster sugar
1 teaspoon imitation vanilla
　essence
80 g unsalted butter, melted
⅔ cup Marsala

½ cup orange marmalade
2 x 250 g punnets strawberries,
　one punnet sliced
2½ cups cream, whipped

Custard
¼ cup custard powder
¼ cup caster sugar
½ cup buttermilk
1 cup milk
1 teaspoon imitation vanilla
　essence
½ cup cream

➤ PREHEAT OVEN to moderate
180°C. Brush a deep, 20 cm round cake

tin with melted butter or with oil.
1 Line base and side with paper;
grease paper. Dust the tin lightly with
flour, shake off excess. Sift dry ingredients three times onto greaseproof
paper. Using electric beaters, beat eggs
in large mixing bowl for 6 minutes or
until thick and pale.
2 Add sugar gradually, beating constantly until dissolved and mixture is
pale and glossy.
Using a metal spoon, fold in essence,
flours and butter quickly and lightly.
Spread mixture evenly into the
prepared tin. Bake for 50 minutes or
until the sponge is lightly golden and

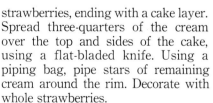

shrinks from side of tin. Leave sponge in tin for 20 minutes before turning onto wire rack to cool.

3 To make Custard: Combine custard powder, sugar, buttermilk and milk in medium pan. Stir continuously over a low heat until mixture boils and thickens. Stir in essence and cream; remove from heat. Cool.

4 Cut cake horizontally into three layers. Brush each layer with Marsala and marmalade. Place first layer on serving plate. Spread cake evenly with half the custard, top with half the sliced strawberries. Continue layering with the remaining cake, custard and strawberries, ending with a cake layer. Spread three-quarters of the cream over the top and sides of the cake, using a flat-bladed knife. Using a piping bag, pipe stars of remaining cream around the rim. Decorate with whole strawberries.

COOK'S FILE

Storage time: This cake is best eaten the day after it is made. This will allow the liqueur to flavour the cake. Cover assembled, undecorated cake with plastic wrap. Store in refrigerator. Decorate the cake with whipped cream and whole strawberries 1 hour before it is served.

Hint: The custard will look curdled until it has boiled and thickened. It will then become smooth and glossy. Buttermilk has a rich, tangy flavour which is particularly appreciated in baked goods. Once, buttermilk was always drawn off butter and slightly soured during the churning. Today, to ensure consistency of product, it is obtained by treating skimmed or partially skimmed milk with a culture of lactic acid bacteria.

VANILLA RASPBERRY CELEBRATION CAKE

Preparation time: 45 minutes
Cooking time: 40 minutes
Makes one 23 cm round cake

150 g unsalted butter
¾ cup caster sugar
2 eggs, lightly beaten
2 teaspoons pure vanilla essence
1 tablespoon glucose syrup
1½ cups self-raising flour
½ cup buttermilk
100 g white chocolate, chopped
2 x 300 g packets frozen
   raspberries, drained, or
   2 punnets fresh raspberries

Vanilla Cream
2 cups cream
2 tablespoons icing sugar
½ teaspoon pure vanilla essence

➤ PREHEAT OVEN to moderate 180°C. Brush a deep, 23 cm round cake tin with melted butter or oil, line base and side with paper; grease paper. Using electric beaters, beat butter and sugar in small mixing bowl until light and creamy.

1 Add the eggs gradually, beating thoroughly after each addition. Add the essence and glucose; beat until combined. Transfer mixture to large mixing bowl. Using a metal spoon, fold in sifted flour alternately with buttermilk. Stir until just combined and the mixture is almost smooth.

2 Pour mixture evenly into prepared tin; smooth surface. Bake 40 minutes or until skewer comes out clean when inserted in centre of cake. Leave cake in tin 15 minutes before turning onto wire rack to cool.

3 Place chocolate in glass bowl. Stir over barely simmering water until melted; remove from heat. Pour chocolate onto a marble or Laminex board in a 4-cm wide strip. Smooth surface. Allow chocolate to set.
Shave off strips with a vegetable peeler. Set aside. (If the weather is very warm, refrigeration may be necessary.)
To make Vanilla Cream: Place cream in small mixing bowl. Using electric beaters, beat until soft peaks form. Add sifted icing sugar and essence. Continue beating until firm peaks form.

4 Cut cake in half horizontally. Place first layer on serving plate. Top with raspberries; slightly squash onto cake with a fork. Sandwich with top cake layer. Spread Vanilla Cream over top and sides of cake using a flat-bladed knife. Smooth surface. Cover cake with white chocolate shavings (see page 11).

COOK'S FILE

Storage time: This cake is best assembled and eaten the day it is made.

COFFEE HAZELNUT MERINGUE TORTE

Preparation time: 1 hour 15 minutes
+ overnight standing
Cooking time: 1 hour
Makes one 20 cm round layer cake

1½ cups/150 g roasted
  hazelnuts
4 egg whites
¾ cup caster sugar
⅓ cup plain flour
1¼ cups cream
1 tablespoon Tia Maria liqueur

Coffee Filling
½ cup caster sugar
2 tablespoons instant coffee
  powder
¼ cup water
4 egg yolks, lightly beaten
250 g unsalted butter, chopped

➤ PREHEAT OVEN to moderately
slow 160°C.
Brush bases of two 20 cm springform
cake tins with melted butter or oil.
Line the bases and sides with paper;
grease paper.
Finely grind hazelnuts in an electric
grinder or food processor. Set aside.
1 Place the egg whites in a small,
clean, dry mixing bowl. Using electric
beaters, beat until firm peaks form.
Add the sugar gradually, beating constantly until dissolved and mixture is
glossy and thick. Transfer mixture to

large mixing bowl; add nuts. Using a
metal spoon, fold in sifted flour. Stir
until just combined.
2 Divide meringue mixture into four
even portions. Spread one portion over
prepared base; smooth surface. Repeat
with second portion. Bake 25 minutes
or until lightly golden and crisp. Alternate trays halfway through cooking.
Leave on trays 3 minutes; lift onto
wire rack to cool. Repeat process with
remaining meringue mixture.
3 To make Coffee Filling: Combine
sugar, coffee powder and water in small
pan. Stir constantly over low heat
until the mixture boils and sugar dissolves. Simmer uncovered, without
stirring, for 5 minutes. Remove from
heat; cool for a further 5 minutes.
Using electric beaters, beat the egg
yolks in small bowl on high speed for
10 minutes. With beaters still operat-
ing, pour warm syrup onto yolks, a
few drops at a time. Continue to beat
until all syrup is added and mixture is
glossy and thick. Beat for 15 minutes
or until the mixture has completely
cooled. Add butter, a piece at a time,
beating thoroughly after each addition.
Place first meringue layer on a serving
plate. Spread evenly with one-third of
the filling. Continue layering with
remaining meringue and filling, and
ending with meringue on top.
4 Whip the cream in a small bowl
until soft peaks form. Fold in liqueur.
Cover the top and sides of the torte
with the whipped cream mixture. Store
in the refrigerator for several hours.

Remove from the refrigerator, leave for
10 minutes before serving.

COOK'S FILE

Storage time: Cake is best assembled
and eaten on the day it is made.
Hint: Cake will cut better and be more
moist if refrigerated for several hours
before serving.
Always add the liqueur after cream
has been whipped. If combined and
whipped together, mixture may curdle.

SUPER-EASY APRICOT AND ALMOND GATEAU

Preparation time: 40 minutes
Cooking time: 40 minutes
Makes one 25 cm oblong cake

¾ cup self-raising flour
¼ cup plain flour
½ cup ground almonds
185 g unsalted butter
1 cup caster sugar
½ cup apricot nectar
3 eggs, lightly beaten
1 x 425 g can apricot halves,
   drained, juice reserved, sliced
2½ cups cream, whipped
½ cup flaked almonds,
   toasted

➤ PREHEAT OVEN to moderate 180˚C. Brush a deep, 25 x 16 x 6 cm loaf tin with melted butter or oil, line base and sides with paper; grease the paper.

1 Sift flours into large mixing bowl. Add ground almonds. Make a well in the centre.
Combine butter, sugar and nectar in a medium pan. Stir over low heat until butter has melted and sugar has dissolved; remove from heat.

2 Add the butter mixture to the dry ingredients. Stir with whisk until just combined. Add eggs; mix well. Pour mixture into prepared tin; smooth the surface. Bake for 40 minutes or until skewer comes out clean when inserted in centre. Leave cake in tin 20 minutes before turning onto wire rack to cool.

3 Cut the cake into three layers horizontally. Brush each layer with the reserved apricot juice.
Sandwich layers together with cream. Using a flat-bladed knife, spread the cream over top and sides of cake.
Carefully press almonds around the sides of the cake. Decorate the top with apricot slices. Using a piping bag, pipe on cream swirls.

COOK'S FILE

Storage time: 2 days in the refrigerator without the toasted almonds. Sprinkle the almonds on just before serving.

Hint: Buy nuts as and when you need them; they quickly spoil and turn rancid, particularly in the heat. Store in an airtight container in a cool place.

CHOCOLATE TRUFFLE CAKE

Preparation time: 2 hours
Cooking time: 30 to 35 minutes
Makes one 20 cm round layer cake

125 g cream cheese, softened
60 g unsalted butter
¾ cup caster sugar
2 eggs, lightly beaten
1 teaspoon imitation vanilla
   essence
¼ teaspoon red food colouring
60 g chocolate, melted
2 cups plain flour
¼ cup cocoa powder
1 teaspoon bicarbonate of soda
¾ cup water

Filling
250 g dark chocolate, chopped
⅓ cup cream
2 egg yolks

Icing
125 g dark chocolate, chopped
125 g unsalted butter

Truffles (makes 20; use 12)
150 g dark chocolate, chopped
50 g unsalted butter
2 tablespoons cream
¼ cup icing sugar
2 teaspoons rum or Grand
   Marnier
⅓ cup cocoa powder
¼ cup drinking chocolate

Chocolate Wedges
150 g dark chocolate, melted

➤ PREHEAT OVEN to moderate 180°C. Brush two deep, 20 cm round cake tins with melted butter or oil, line bases and sides with paper; grease the paper.

1 Using electric beaters, beat the cream cheese, butter and sugar in small mixing bowl until light and creamy. Add eggs gradually, beating thoroughly after each addition. Add essence, colouring and chocolate; beat until combined.
Transfer the mixture to a large mixing bowl. Using a metal spoon, fold in sifted flour, cocoa and soda alternately with water. Stir until just combined and the mixture is almost smooth.
Pour mixture evenly into prepared tins. Smooth surfaces; bake cakes for 30 to 35 minutes or until skewer comes out clean when inserted in centres of cakes. Leave cakes in tins 10 minutes before turning onto wire rack to cool.
2 To make Filling: Combine the chocolate and cream in a small pan. Stir over low heat until chocolate has melted; remove from heat. Whisk in egg yolks until mixture is smooth. Set aside.
3 To make Icing: Place the chocolate in a glass bowl. Stir over barely simmering water until melted; remove from heat. Beat the butter in a small mixing bowl until light and creamy. Add the chocolate, beating 1 minute or until the mixture is glossy and smooth. Set mixture aside.
4 To make Truffles: Combine the chocolate, butter, cream, sifted icing sugar and the liqueur in a small pan. Stir over low heat until chocolate and butter have melted; remove from heat. Transfer mixture to medium mixing bowl. Refrigerate for 15 minutes or until semi-set. Using electric beaters, beat the mixture until it is creamy.
Roll heaped teaspoonfuls of mixture into balls; roll in combined sifted cocoa and drinking chocolate to coat. Refrigerate until firm.
5 To make Chocolate Wedges: Cover the base of a 20 cm round cake tin with foil. Spread melted chocolate evenly over the foil, refrigerate until it is semi-set.

Using a sharp, flat-bladed knife, carefully mark chocolate into 12 wedges. Return to refrigerator until chocolate is completely set.
6 To assemble, cut the domes off both the cakes to give a level surface. Cut

1

2

3

each cake in half horizontally. Place first cake layer on serving plate. Spread cake evenly with one third of the filling. Continue layering with the remaining cake and filling, ending with a cake layer on top.

Spread the icing evenly over top and side of cake using a flat-bladed knife. Decorate the top by placing 12 truffles around the rim of the cake. Position the chocolate wedges on cake, resting each one on a truffle.

COOK'S FILE

Storage time: Up to 4 days in the refrigerator.
Hint: Have cream cheese at room temperature to make it easier to work.

4

5

6

1

2

3

CHOCOLATE MOUSSE TORTE

Preparation time: 1 hour 30 minutes
+ 4 hours standing
Cooking time: 15 minutes
Makes one 20 cm square layer cake

4 eggs, separated
¼ cup icing sugar
½ cup self-raising flour
⅓ cup ground walnuts
200 g dark chocolate, chopped
2 tablespoons cocoa powder
1 tablespoon drinking chocolate
fresh berries, for decoration

Chocolate Mousse
100 g white chocolate, chopped
2 egg whites
2 tablespoons icing sugar
2 teaspoons gelatine
1 tablespoon hot water
1¼ cups cream, whipped
¾ cup grated milk chocolate

➤ PREHEAT OVEN to moderate 180°C. Brush two deep, 20 cm square cake tins with melted butter or oil, line bases and sides with paper; grease paper. Dust tins lightly with flour, shake off excess.

1 Place egg whites in small, clean, dry mixing bowl. Using electric beaters, beat until firm peaks form. Add the sifted icing sugar gradually, beating constantly until dissolved and mixture is glossy and thick. Add the beaten egg yolks; beat further 20 seconds. Transfer mixture to large mixing bowl.

2 Using a metal spoon, fold in sifted flour and walnuts quickly and lightly. Spread mixture evenly into prepared tins. Bake for 15 minutes or until the sponges are lightly golden and have shrunk from sides of tins. Leave in tins

for 5 minutes before turning onto wire rack to cool.

3 To make Chocolate Mousse: Place chocolate in glass bowl. Stir over barely simmering water until melted; remove from heat.

Place egg whites in small, clean, dry mixing bowl. Using electric beaters, beat until firm peaks form. Add sifted icing sugar gradually, beating constantly until dissolved. Combine gelatine with water in a small bowl. Stand bowl in hot water; stir until dissolved.

Pour gelatine mixture in a thin stream over egg whites, beating constantly until well combined. Transfer mixture to large mixing bowl. Using a metal spoon, fold in chocolate, cream and grated chocolate.

4 Line a deep, 20 cm square tin with paper. Place one sponge in the base of tin. Pour mousse over the top; smooth surface. Place the second sponge on the top. Cover with plastic wrap, refrigerate for 4 hours or until set.

5 Melt chopped dark chocolate as for Step 3. Cover the base of a 32 x 28 cm oven tray with foil. Spread chocolate evenly over foil to cover the base of tray, swirl waves with the tines of a fork. Refrigerate until partially set. Carefully mark 6 cm squares with a sharp, clean, flat-bladed knife. You will need 20 squares for decoration. Return tray to the refrigerator until chocolate is completely set.

6 Lift cake from tin, using the lining paper to help. Carefully press the chocolate squares around the edges, overlapping each one. Sprinkle top of cake liberally with combined sifted cocoa and drinking chocolate. Decorate with fresh berries or seasonal fruits of your choice.

COOK'S FILE

Storage time: 1 day in the refrigerator.

4

5

6

STRAWBERRY CHARLOTTE RUSSE

Preparation time: 1 hour
Cooking time: 20 minutes
+ 2 hours setting
Makes one 20 cm round cake

4 eggs, separated
¼ cup caster sugar
1 teaspoon imitation vanilla
   essence
½ cup self-raising flour
¼ cup plain flour
¼ cup desiccated coconut
110 g jar blackcurrant baby gel
2 x 125 g packets small sponge
   fingers

Strawberry Mousse
1 tablespoon gelatine
¼ cup orange juice
2 x 250 g punnets strawberries
⅓ cup caster sugar
1 tablespoon cream
2 eggs, separated
1¼ cups cream, whipped

➤ PREHEAT OVEN to moderate 180°C.
1 Brush a deep, 20 cm round springform tin with melted butter or oil, line base and side with paper; grease paper. Dust tin lightly with flour, shake off excess. Sift the flours three times onto greaseproof paper. Place egg whites in a small, clean, dry mixing bowl. Using electric beaters, beat until firm peaks form. Add sugar gradually, beating constantly until dissolved and mixture is glossy and thick.
2 Add the beaten egg yolks; beat for a further 20 seconds. Transfer mixture to large mixing bowl.
Using a metal spoon, fold in essence, flours and coconut quickly and lightly. Spread mixture evenly into prepared tin. Bake for 20 minutes or until the sponge is lightly golden and has shrunk from side of tin. Leave sponge in tin 10 minutes before turning onto wire rack to cool.
3 To make Strawberry Mousse: Combine gelatine with orange juice in small bowl. Stand bowl in hot water; stir until mixture dissolves.
Place one punnet of strawberries, the sugar, gelatine mixture, cream and egg yolks in food-processor bowl. Using the pulse action, press button for 20 seconds or until mixture is smooth. Transfer mixture to a large mixing bowl. Using a metal spoon, fold in whipped cream. Place egg whites in small, clean, dry mixer bowl. Beat with electric beaters until soft peaks form. Fold into strawberry mixture.
Reline springform tin with paper. Cut dome off cake horizontally to give a level surface. Place cake in lined tin. Pour mousse evenly into prepared tin

to cover cake. Cover, refrigerate several hours or until set.
4 Place the baby gel in a small pan. Stir over a low heat until melted; remove pan from the heat. Decorate the top of the mousse with remaining

strawberries. Brush with baby gel until well coated. Remove cake from the tin. Place on a serving plate. Cut sponge fingers to the height of the cake. Press carefully around edges of cake. Secure with a ribbon if desired.

COOK'S FILE

Storage time: Up to 3 days in the refrigerator without the addition of the sponge fingers; add the fingers just before serving.

Hint: For an attractive finish, baby gel makes an excellent, 'ready-made' glaze. You will find it is sold in small jars in the baby food section of your supermarket. It is also available in flavours other than blackcurrant.

111

SACHER TORTE

Preparation time: 40 minutes
Cooking time: 50 minutes
Makes one 20 cm round cake

1 cup plain flour
¼ cup cocoa powder
1 cup caster sugar
100 g unsalted butter
2 tablespoons strawberry jam
4 eggs, separated
2 tablespoons strawberry jam,
   extra, melted

Ganache Topping
150 g dark chocolate, chopped
¼ cup cream

➤ PREHEAT OVEN to moderate 180°C. Brush a deep, 20 cm round cake tin with melted butter or oil, line the base and side with paper; grease the paper.

1 Sift the flour and cocoa into a large mixing bowl. Make a well in the centre. Combine sugar, butter and jam in small pan. Stir over low heat until the butter has melted and sugar has dissolved; remove from heat.

Add butter mixture to dry ingredients. Using a whisk, stir until just combined; add egg yolks, mix well.

2 Place egg whites in small, clean, dry mixing bowl. Using electric beaters, beat until soft peaks form. Using a metal spoon, fold egg whites into cake mixture.

Pour mixture into the prepared tin; smooth surface. Bake 50 minutes or until skewer comes out clean when inserted in centre of cake. Leave cake in tin 15 minutes before turning onto wire rack to cool.

3 To make Ganache Topping: Combine chocolate and cream in small pan. Stir over low heat until chocolate has melted and mixture is smooth. Remove from heat. Cool.

Cut the dome off the top of the cake horizontally. Turn the cake so that the base side is up. Brush cake with extra jam. Place on a wire rack set over a baking tray.

4 Pour Ganache Topping completely over cake. Smooth top and sides using a flat-bladed knife. Place remaining mixture in a piping bag and pipe the words 'Sacher Torte' across the top of the cake. Allow to set. Transfer cake carefully to serving plate.

COOK'S FILE

Storage time: 1 week in an airtight container or up to 3 months in the freezer uniced.

Biscuit Basics

Baking biscuits and slices is fun – and your efforts will be rewarded by the appreciation of your family and friends. You'll find the job much easier if you are properly prepared before you start. Here is an outline of the equipment you need, and tips on methods and ingredients.

Although it is not strictly necessary for successful baking to have a perfectly equipped kitchen, it does make the job easier and the results more reliable. For example, using the tin size specified in a slice recipe will take the guesswork out of both the cooking time and the number of pieces the recipe makes.

Ovens

An accurate oven is probably the most important piece of equipment for baking. All ovens are different, and not all thermometers are reliable. When you know your oven well, you will be able to make small adjustments to time and temperature if necessary. If you find a big variation, have your oven checked – it can lose its calibration.

Unless a recipe includes a waiting time (for example, pastry that has to be chilled in the refrigerator for a long period), turn on the oven before you begin your preparations.

For best results with biscuits and slices, put the oven rack in the middle of the oven. With cakes, the rack should be placed lower, so that the top of the cake is approximately in the middle. If you are using two tins or trays at the same time, stagger them so one is not directly above the other. Halfway through the cooking time, swap their positions. You may have to add a minute or two to the cooking time.

If both tins fit on the same rack, place them away from the sides and back of the oven. During the last third of the cooking time, check to see if they need turning to give an even result.

Beaters and processors

An electric beater allows you to cream butter and sugar easily to the right consistency. It also beats egg whites and egg white mixtures quickly. A hand-held electric beater will do the same job, provided quantities are not too great. However, mixing time will be increased considerably.

Food processors are ideal for blending ingredients, but are unsuitable for creaming mixtures, beating egg whites or whipping cream.

Measuring cups and spoons

Metric measuring cups and spoons are important for accurate results. For dry ingredients, you'll need four standard metric measuring cups – one cup, half cup, one-third cup and quarter cup. To measure, place the cup on a flat surface, spoon the dry ingredient – such as flour or sugar – lightly into it, and level off the surface with a knife. Don't press or shake down the ingredient you're measuring. The exception is soft brown sugar, which should be packed down tightly into the cup and levelled off at the top.

For liquid ingredients, you need a 250 mL metric measuring cup or 1-litre jug. Choose one made of glass or heatproof plastic, with a pouring lip (glass is easier to use, as you can clearly see the level of the liquid you are measuring). Place the cup or jug on a board, add the required amount of liquid, and check the measurement marks down the side.

Measuring spoons are another essential for accurately measuring small quantities of liquid and dry ingredients – everyday tableware is a different size. You will need one tablespoon, one teaspoon, half teaspoon and quarter teaspoon sizes.

Place dry ingredient in a measuring cup. Level with a knife.

Pack soft brown sugar into measuring cup; press down with back of spoon.

To measure liquid, place jug on flat surface. Measure liquid at eye level.

Place the dry ingredient in measuring spoon. Level with a knife.

Steps to successful baking

☐ Read through the recipe first, then gather the equipment and ingredients you'll need. Use room-temperature ingredients unless otherwise specified.

☐ Preheat the oven to the desired temperature, checking that the oven rack is in the position you want it. Prepare tins or trays.

☐ Measure ingredients accurately, with standard metric measuring cups and spoons.

☐ Sift dry ingredients.

☐ Cream butter and sugar mixtures thoroughly.

☐ Avoid opening the oven door until at least two-thirds of the way through baking.

☐ Test slices in the centre with a skewer for doneness a few minutes before the end of suggested cooking time.

☐ Stand biscuits or slices in tins or on trays for the specified time before cooling.

☐ Transfer to a wire rack to cool completely.

☐ Remove baked slice from tin before you cut it. This makes it possible for you to cut it into even slices without the pan getting in the way.

Kitchen scales provide the easiest way to measure butter.

To measure a dry ingredient, fill the spoon and level it off with a knife. Simply pour liquids in until they are level with the top of the spoon.

Scales

Kitchen scales can be a useful cooking aid, particularly for large quantities of ingredients such as dried fruit, chocolate, nuts and so on, but are not essential. They are handy for measuring butter, but some packets of butter have weight markings on the side of the wrapper.

If you do have scales, and prefer to measure by weight rather than volume, you'll find a conversion chart for metric cup measures on page 112.

Baking equipment

Basic baking equipment specifically for biscuits and slices includes oven or biscuit trays, shallow square and rectangular tins, bar tins and Swiss roll tins.

Standard size tins and trays used in our recipes are:

32 x 28 cm biscuit trays

30 x 20 cm and 27 x 18 cm shallow rectangular cake tins

30 x 25 cm Swiss roll tin

23 cm square shallow cake tin

23 cm fluted round loose-bottomed flan tin

26 x 8 x 4.5 cm bar tin.

If these sizes are not available, use the nearest size you have. Cooking times may vary slightly.

Useful extras are wire cake racks for cooling biscuits and slices; wire sifters; a selection of wooden and metal spoons; a range of mixing bowls, preferably glass; rubber and plastic spatulas and sharp and flat-bladed knives.

Types of biscuits and slices

Biscuits and slices fall into several different categories, depending on the way they are made.

☐ Slices are made from a fairly firm dough which is spread or pressed into a tin, or a softer batter-type mixture which can be poured into the tin. They vary in texture from chewy to cakelike and can be cut into various shapes – squares, bars, diamonds and triangles.

☐ Cut-out biscuits are made from a fairly soft dough which may be chilled, then rolled out and cut into shapes, such as gingerbread people. Thinly rolled biscuits will be crisper than thicker varieties.

☐ Some biscuits, such as chocolate chip cookies and macaroons, are made from a soft dough which is dropped in teaspoonfuls onto a biscuit tray. Their texture can be crisp, chewy or cakelike.

☐ Shaped biscuits are made from a firm dough which may need to be refrigerated before shaping. They are moulded by hand or shaped with a utensil such as the bottom of a glass, a fork or a biscuit mould.

☐ Sliced biscuits are made from a softish dough, shaped into a roll, then refrigerated before it is sliced into rounds and baked. Sliced biscuits are crisp but tender.

☐ Shortbread is made from a type of pastry dough, and is buttery and crisp in texture. It may be kneaded and rolled out or pressed into a tin, and cut into triangles or bars.

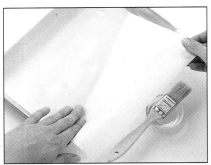

To line slice tin, cut a piece of paper that will overhang on two sides.

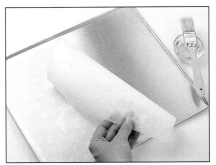

To line biscuit tray, cut paper just to fit the bottom of the tray.

Preparing tins and trays

Preparation of tins and trays depends on the type of biscuit or slice you are baking, and will be specified in the recipe. Have the tin ready before you begin, to avoid last-minute panic.

To grease a biscuit tin or tray, use melted, unsalted butter or oil. Use a pastry brush to spread it on evenly and not too thickly. Alternatively, you can use a vegetable baking spray; apply it in a well-ventilated area away from heat.

Greaseproof paper is good to use for lining tins. Non-stick baking paper also works well, and does not need to be greased.

To line base and sides of a tin, place its base on a square of paper and trace around the outside. Measure the depth of the tin, then measure paper from the marked line and cut all around to 2 cm larger than the depth.

Crease paper along marked lines and cut the paper diagonally from outside edge to each corner. After greasing the tin, press the paper down into its base and sides. Sometimes the recipe specifies lining the base and two opposite sides of a tin. This is so the slice can easily be lifted out and requires one continuous sheet of paper.

If the tin or paper needs to be dusted, let the butter or oil dry off a little first. Use plain flour, and turn the tin to coat sides and base evenly. Shake off the excess before using. Some recipes call for the tin to be dusted with desiccated coconut, fine breadcrumbs or nuts. This is done in the same way.

Ingredients

Each ingredient used in baking has a specific purpose.

Flour: Plain and self-raising flours are used in our recipes. Plain flour has no raising agent. To use plain instead of self-raising, add 2 standard metric teaspoons baking powder to each 3/4 standard metric cup of plain flour. Sift flour and baking powder together three times before using.

Eggs: These bind the other ingredients together. We have used 60 g eggs. For baking, eggs should be at room temperature; take them out of the refrigerator an hour before using. However, eggs separate more easily when cold.

Butter: Butter supplies flavour, texture and aroma. Unsalted butter gives a fuller, richer and sweeter flavour. Butter should be at room temperature for it to cream properly. If it is too cold, it will not aerate well; if it is soft and oily it will not aerate at all.

Sugar: Sugar tenderises, and adds sweetness and colour. Fine textured caster sugar is commonly used in baking. Granulated everyday sugar is more difficult to cream, and produces a coarser textured result. Soft brown sugar is also frequently used in these recipes; use soft dark brown sugar for a more intense flavour, if preferred.

Milk: This is the liquid most commonly used in baking.

Flavourings and essences: These should be of good quality. Pure vanilla essence is very expensive and hard to find; imitation vanilla essence is more commonly used. This varies considerably in strength, so it may be necessary to experiment with quantities.

Fruits and nuts: A large variety of chopped and ground nuts and dried and glacé fruits can be used, as well as some tinned fruits. When grating orange or lemon rind, grate only the coloured surface of the skin, not the white, bitter pith.

Making shortbread on a mould

Dust the mould with cornflour, then sprinkle with sugar. Press the shortbread dough onto the mould and trim off the excess with a sharp knife. Refrigerate for 30 minutes. Tap the mould sharply and turn out onto a paper-lined surface, then transfer to a baking tray. Do not wash the mould after use; if any bits of shortbread remain on it, remove them by brushing with a dry pastry brush.

Biscuit-making methods

Melt and mix method: Mix together dry ingredients. Melt the butter and add it to the dry ingredients. Stir with a wooden spoon until the dry ingredients have incorporated the melted butter. The mixture will be fairly dry and is usually formed into balls or other shapes with the hands.

Processor method: The dry ingredients are placed in the food processor with chopped butter. The mixture is processed only until it comes together in a mass. Over-processing will toughen the biscuits.

Creaming method: An electric mixer produces the best biscuits made by the creaming method. The butter is cut into pieces and put into a bowl with the sugar. The mixture is creamed together until light and fluffy and almost white. For the best results, cream the butter and sugar well.

Rubbing-in method: This can be done by hand or in a food processor. The butter is cut into small pieces and is rubbed into the flour with just the fingertips until the mixture resembles fine or coarse breadcrumbs (depending on the recipe). It should be done quickly and with cool hands.

Rolling the dough: Because biscuit dough contains a lot of butter, it may have to be rolled between plastic wrap or greaseproof paper to prevent it from sticking to board and rolling pin, and to make it unnecessary to use extra flour which would change the texture of the biscuits. Lay dough on a sheet of plastic wrap or greaseproof paper placed on a board or marble slab. Cover with another sheet and roll out, turning pastry and paper a quarter turn after each roll.

Kneading the dough: Some biscuit dough has to be kneaded, although generally the less the dough is handled, the lighter the biscuit. When dough is to be kneaded, place it on a flat board or marble slab. Flour the board lightly – if you use too much flour, it will be absorbed into the dough and the biscuits will be drier. Form the dough into a round and push it with the heel of your hand into the thickness required.

Drop soft dough in spoonfuls onto prepared baking tray.

Use a piping bag to make neatly shaped finger biscuits.

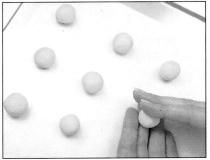

Roll firmer dough into even balls with your fingertips.

Use a fluted pastry wheel to achieve an attractive finish to edges.

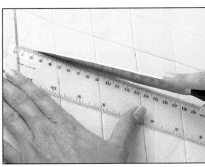

Cut dough into evenly-sized diamonds with a sharp knife and ruler.

Roll firm dough into sausages and twist into pretzels or knots.

Shaping biscuits

Soft biscuit doughs are usually dropped by the spoonful onto biscuit trays or piped with a piping bag, but the firmer doughs can be shaped before baking. They can be formed into balls and left to spread out during baking, or the balls can be flattened with the base of a glass to produce a more even result. The firmer doughs can be twisted into little pretzels or knots, or they can be cut with shaped cutters into stars, crescents, hearts, diamonds and so on.

A pastry wheel can be used to give a pretty edging on square or rectangular biscuits, and cutting with a knife and ruler will produce really sharp edges, which are especially necessary for diamonds.

Shaped biscuits are cooked when the edges are firm and the bottoms are lightly browned.

Storing

Most biscuits can be kept for two to three days in an airtight jar or airtight plastic container. Allow them to cool before storing. Biscuits with fancy decorations are best stored in layers, with a sheet of greaseproof paper between each layer. Leave sufficient space to close the container without damaging the biscuits.

Store the container in a cool dry place, unless refrigeration is specified in the recipe. Unbaked slices which may contain gelatine will need to be kept in the refrigerator.

Except in very hot weather, it is unnecessary to keep chocolate-decorated biscuits and slices in the refrigerator.

Freezing biscuits

If well wrapped, biscuit dough can be frozen for up to six months. Meringue-type mixtures and very thin batters do not freeze well. Thaw frozen biscuit dough thoroughly before baking. Biscuit dough that has been formed into a roll should be cut into slices when still partially frozen. If left to soften, it won't slice evenly.

To freeze cooked biscuits, allow them to cool and store them without icing. Arrange them in a single layer in an airtight container and cover with a layer of greaseproof paper. Repeat layers of biscuits and paper, seal tightly and freeze for up to four to six months. Biscuits can also be frozen in small batches in plastic bags.

Store biscuits in an airtight plastic or glass container.

Decorating biscuits and slices

The simplest way to decorate biscuits is to dust them with sieved icing sugar. For many biscuits, any additional decoration is unnecessary.

Soft butter icing can be piped onto the top of biscuits, or spread with a flat-bladed knife. Thin icings can be spread on with a knife or the biscuit can be dipped into the icing (either one side or one half).

Most filled biscuits are filled with a soft buttery icing and are usually spread over one biscuit then sandwiched with another.

Chocolate is a very convenient icing for biscuits and slices. Biscuits can be dipped into melted chocolate (once again, dip one side in, or half of a whole biscuit – one half could be dark chocolate, the other half white chocolate, if desired). Melted chocolate, either white, milk or dark, can be spooned into an icing bag and piped in a pattern over the top of your biscuits. To melt chocolate, chop into even-sized pieces and place in glass bowl over a pan of simmering water. Stir gently until chocolate has melted. Do not allow any water to fall on the chocolate, or it will become unworkable.

Piping bags

A piping bag is an ideal tool to use when working with fine icing and when icing biscuits with melted chocolate. You can easily make your own.

Cut a 25 cm square of strong greaseproof paper and fold it in half diagonally to form a triangle. Working with the long side at the bottom, roll a corner to the centre and tape it in place. Use scissors to snip off the end of the bag to suit the size of the decorating you will be doing. You can also drop a small nozzle into the bag for icing.

Using a knife or metal spatula, half-fill the bag with melted chocolate or icing. Fold in the top, then roll the top down to the level of the icing to seal the bag. With your writing hand, grip the bag at the top with the full end resting in your palm. Use pressure from the palm of your hand to push the icing through the hole. Practice will show how to vary the pressure and achieve a good flow of icing.

An alternative method of piping is to use purchased piping bags, available from specialty kitchen shops. These fabric or thermoplastic bags are used with metal or plastic nozzles. Some of the smaller metal nozzles have a screw attachment which allows you to use several different shaped nozzles without having to transfer icing to a new bag.

Spread biscuits with buttercream and sandwich together.

Dip the base of biscuits into melted white, milk or dark chocolate.

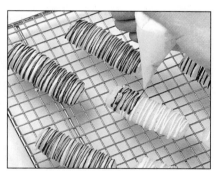

Pipe alternate rows of white and dark chocolate onto biscuits.

Dip the top of biscuits into glacé icing for an easy finish.

Use a flat-bladed knife to spread icing on top of biscuits.

Use a fine sieve to dust biscuits with icing sugar.

Mouthwatering CLASSICS

RASPBERRY COCONUT BISCUITS

Preparation time: 40 minutes
Total cooking time: 10 minutes each tray
Makes 28

Biscuit Pastry
60 g butter
1/2 cup caster sugar
1 egg
2/3 cup plain flour
2/3 cup self-raising flour

Icing
100 g packet pink marshmallows
40 g butter
1/4 cup icing sugar, sifted
1/2 cup desiccated coconut
1/3 cup raspberry jam

➤ PREHEAT OVEN to moderate 180°C. Line two oven trays with baking paper.

1 To make Pastry: Using electric beaters, beat the butter and sugar in small mixing bowl until light and creamy. Transfer to large bowl. Add egg; beat until combined. Using a metal spoon, fold in sifted flours. Turn dough onto lightly floured surface. Knead gently for 1 minute or until smooth. Roll out dough between baking paper to 4 mm thickness. Using a knife or fluted pastry wheel, cut dough into 4.5 x 6 cm rectangles. Place on prepared trays, allowing room for spreading. Re-roll remaining pastry and repeat cutting. Bake for 10 minutes or until lightly golden. Transfer to wire rack when cool.

2 To make Icing: Combine marshmallows and butter in small pan. Stir over low heat until marshmallows and butter are melted and smooth. Stir in icing sugar; mix until smooth. Place coconut on sheet of greaseproof paper. Working quickly, spread about quarter teaspoon of icing along each long side of biscuit, leaving a space in the centre. Dip iced biscuit into coconut; shake off excess coconut.

3 Place jam in small pan and heat gently until thinned and warm. Spread a little jam down centre of each biscuit.

COOK'S FILE

Storage time: Biscuits can be kept for three days in a single layer in an airtight container.

Hint: Stand icing in bowl of hot water while icing biscuits, to prevent it from setting too quickly.

Variation: For a totally different look, use white marshmallows and apricot jam.

CHINESE FORTUNE COOKIES

Preparation time: 15 minutes
Total cooking time: About 5 minutes
each tray
Makes about 30

3 egg whites
1/2 cup icing sugar, sifted
**45 g unsalted butter,
melted**
1/2 cup plain flour

➤ PREHEAT OVEN to moderate 180°C. Line oven tray with baking paper. Draw three 8 cm circles on the paper.
1 Place egg whites in medium bowl and whisk until just frothy. Add icing sugar and butter and stir until smooth. Add flour; mix until smooth and stand 15 minutes. Using a flat-bladed knife, spread 1 1/2 level tea-spoons of mixture over each circle. Bake 5 minutes or until slightly brown around the edges.
2 Working quickly, remove from

trays by sliding a flat-bladed knife under each round; place a written fortune message in each cookie.
3 Fold in half, then in half again over a blunt-edged object. Allow to cool on wire rack. Cook remaining mixture the same way.

COOK'S FILE

Storage time: Store up to two days in an airtight container.
Hint: Make cookies two or three at a time; otherwise they will harden too quickly and break when folding.

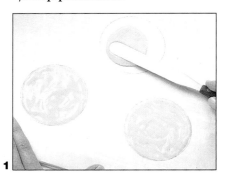

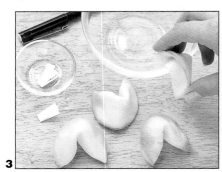

CHOCOLATE CHIP COOKIES

Preparation time: 10 minutes
Total cooking time: 15 minutes
Makes 24

150 g unsalted butter
1/4 cup soft brown
    sugar
1/3 cup caster sugar
1 egg yolk
1 teaspoon vanilla
    essence
1 1/2 cups self-raising
    flour
1 cup (200 g) choc dots

➤ PREHEAT OVEN to moderate 180°C. Line a 32 x 28 cm biscuit tray with baking paper.

1 Using electric beaters, beat butter, sugars and yolk in small mixing bowl until light and creamy. Add essence, beat until combined.

2 Transfer mixture to large mixing bowl; add flour and two-thirds of the dots. Using a metal spoon, stir until ingredients are just combined.

3 Using fingers, press mixture together to form a soft dough. Roll one tablespoon of mixture at a time into a ball.

4 Press remaining chocolate dots firmly on top of balls. Arrange on prepared tray, allowing room for spreading. Bake 15 minutes or until crisp and lightly browned. Cool biscuits on trays.

COOK'S FILE

Storage time: Store biscuits in an airtight container for up to three days.

Hint: Choc dots are a smaller version of choc bits. Use choc bits in place of choc dots if preferred. Alternatively, use half chopped white chocolate and any selection of chopped nuts.

CHOCOLATE FUDGE BROWNIES

Preparation time: 15 minutes +
  1 hour refrigeration
Total cooking time: 12 minutes
Makes 30

3/4 cup plain flour
1/2 cup self-raising flour
1 cup (130 g) chopped walnuts
1/2 cup choc bits
125 g unsalted butter,
  chopped
200 g dark chocolate, chopped
2 tablespoons golden syrup
2 eggs, lightly beaten

➤ LINE A 32 x 28 cm biscuit tray with baking paper.

1 Sift plain and self-raising flours into a large mixing bowl; add walnuts and choc bits. Make a well in the centre.

2 Combine pieces of butter and chocolate in small pan. Stir over low heat for 5 minutes or until chocolate has melted and the mixture is smooth. Remove pan from heat; add syrup and beaten eggs, mix well.

3 Pour chocolate mixture into large mixing bowl with the dry ingredients. Using a metal spoon, stir until just combined. Cover the mixture with plastic wrap and refrigerate for 1 hour.

4 Heat oven to moderate 180°C. Roll 1 level tablespoon of mixture at a time into a ball. Arrange balls on the prepared tray; bake for 12 minutes. (The biscuits will still be soft at this stage; they will become firm on standing). Remove biscuits from oven; transfer to a wire rack to cool.

COOK'S FILE

Storage time: Biscuits may be stored in an airtight container for up to two days.

Hint: These rich chocolate brownies have a fudge-like texture. Sprinkle brownies with chocolate sprinkles before baking if liked.

Variation: This brownie mixture can also be baked in a tin as a slice and cut into fingers when cooked. Spread with your favourite rich chocolate icing before cutting, if desired.

ALMOND CINNAMON BISCUITS

Preparation time: 12 minutes
Total cooking time: 20 minutes
Makes 45

200 g blanched almonds
1/3 cup caster sugar
1/3 cup icing sugar
**3 teaspoons ground
cinnamon**
3/4 cup plain flour
2 egg whites

Vanilla Icing
1 2/3 cups pure icing sugar
1 egg white, lightly beaten
1/2 teaspoon vanilla essence

➤ PREHEAT OVEN to slow 150°C. Line a 32 x 28 cm biscuit tray with baking paper.

1 Place almonds, sugars, cinnamon and flour in food processor bowl. Using pulse action, press button for 30 seconds or until mixture is fine and crumbly. Add egg whites; process 30 seconds or until a soft dough forms.

2 Turn dough onto lightly floured surface. Knead for 1 minute; shape into a ball. Roll dough between two sheets of plastic wrap to 5 mm thickness. Cut into shapes, using a 4 cm plain or fluted biscuit cutter; place on prepared tray. Bake 20 minutes or until golden. Transfer biscuits to wire rack to cool.

3 **To make Vanilla Icing:** Sift icing sugar into a small mixing bowl. Make a well in centre; add combined egg white and essence. Beat constantly with a wooden spoon until all the icing sugar is incorporated and a firm paste is formed. Using a flat-bladed knife, spread biscuits with vanilla icing.

COOK'S FILE

Storage time: Biscuits may be stored in an airtight container for up to two days.

Variations: Use 1 teaspoon ground nutmeg in place of the cinnamon if preferred. Spread biscuits with lemon icing instead of vanilla, if preferred. Simply add 2 teaspoons of finely grated lemon rind in place of vanilla essence.

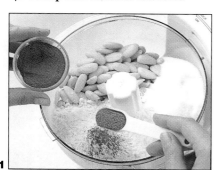

1

2

3

LEBKUCHEN

Preparation time: 25 minutes
Total cooking time: 25 minutes
Makes 35

2¹/3 cups plain flour
¹/2 cup cornflour
2 teaspoons cocoa powder
1 teaspoon mixed spice
1 teaspoon ground
   cinnamon
¹/2 teaspoon ground nutmeg
100 g unsalted butter
³/4 cup golden syrup
2 tablespoons milk
150 g white chocolate melts
¹/4 teaspoon mixed spice, extra

➤ PREHEAT OVEN to moderate 180°C. Line a 32 x 28 cm biscuit tray with baking paper.

1 Sift flours, cocoa and spices into a large mixing bowl. Make well in centre.

2 Combine butter, syrup and milk in small pan. Stir over low heat until butter is melted and mixture smooth; remove from heat.

3 Add butter mixture to dry ingredients. Using a flat-bladed knife, stir well until a soft dough is formed. Turn dough onto lightly floured surface. Knead for 1 minute until smooth. Shape dough into a ball.

4 Roll dough to 7 mm thickness. Cut into heart shapes using a 6 cm biscuit cutter. Place on prepared tray; bake 25 minutes or until lightly browned. Cool on wire rack.

5 Place chocolate in small heatproof bowl. Stand over pan of simmering water and stir until melted. Remove from heat.

6 Dip one side of biscuits into chocolate. Place biscuits onto greaseproof paper until chocolate has set. Sprinkle with mixed spice.

COOK'S FILE

Storage time: Store biscuits in an airtight container for up to two days.

SCOTCH OATCAKES

Preparation time: 12 minutes
Total cooking time: 20 minutes
Makes 30 triangles

2/3 cup plain flour
1/2 teaspoon bicarbonate of soda
2 1/2 cups oatbran
1/3 cup caster sugar
150 g unsalted butter, melted
1 egg, lightly beaten

➤ PREHEAT OVEN to moderate 180°C. Line a 32 x 28 cm biscuit tray with baking paper.

1 Sift flour with remaining dry ingredients into large mixing bowl. Make a well in the centre. Add combined butter and egg mixture to dry ingredients. Using a wooden spoon, stir until the ingredients are just combined.

2 Press mixture firmly into a foil-lined, shallow 30 x 20 cm rectangular cake tin. Turn out onto a board. Cut into 15 squares, then cut diagonally across the squares to make 30 triangles.

3 Arrange biscuits on prepared tray. Bake 20 minutes or until lightly browned. Cool biscuits on tray.

COOK'S FILE

Storage time: Biscuits may be stored in an airtight container for up to two days.

Hint: Oatbran may be found in supermarkets and health food shops.

1

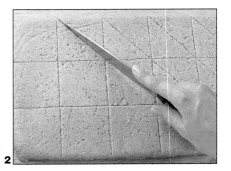

2

3

VIENNESE FINGERS

Preparation time: 15 minutes
Total cooking time: 12 minutes
Makes 20

100 g unsalted butter
¹/3 cup icing sugar
2 egg yolks
1¹/2 teaspoons vanilla
  essence
1 cup plain flour
100 g dark cooking chocolate,
  grated
30 g butter

➤ PREHEAT OVEN to moderate 180°C. Brush a 32 x 28 cm biscuit tray with melted butter or oil, line base with paper; grease paper.

1 Using electric beaters, beat butter and sugar in small mixing bowl until light and creamy. Add egg yolks and essence and beat thoroughly. Transfer mixture to a large mixing bowl; add flour. Using a metal spoon, stir until ingredients are just combined and mixture is smooth.

2 Spoon mixture into a piping bag fitted with fluted 1 cm piping nozzle; pipe mixture into wavy 6 cm lengths on prepared tray. Bake 12 minutes until lightly golden. Transfer biscuits to wire rack to cool.

3 Place chocolate and butter in small heatproof bowl. Stand over pan of simmering water and stir until chocolate is melted and mixture smooth. Dip half of each biscuit into melted chocolate; allow to set on greaseproof paper.

COOK'S FILE

Storage time: Biscuits may be stored in an airtight container for up to two days.

Hint: Dust biscuits with icing sugar before serving.

AMARETTI

Preparation time: 15 minutes +
  1 hour standing
Total cooking time: 20 minutes
Makes 40

1 tablespoon plain flour
1 tablespoon cornflour
1 teaspoon ground cinnamon
2/3 cup caster sugar
1 teaspoon grated lemon rind
1 cup (120 g) ground almonds
2 egg whites
1/4 cup icing sugar

➤ LINE A 32 x 28 cm biscuit tray with baking paper.

1 Sift plain flour, cornflour, cinnamon and half the sugar into a large bowl; add lemon rind and ground almonds.

2 Place the egg whites in small, dry mixing bowl. Using electric beaters, beat egg whites until firm peaks form. Add reserved one-third cup sugar gradually, beating constantly until the mixture is thick and glossy and all the sugar has dissolved. Using a metal spoon, fold egg white mixture into dry ingredients. Stir until ingredients are just combined and mixture forms a soft dough.

3 Roll 2 level teaspoons of mixture at a time with oiled or wetted hands into a ball. Arrange on prepared tray, allowing room for spreading. Set tray aside, uncovered, for 1 hour before baking.

4 Heat oven to moderate 180°C. Sift icing sugar liberally over the biscuits. Bake for 15–20 minutes or until crisp and lightly browned. Transfer biscuits to wire rack to cool.

COOK'S FILE

Storage time: Biscuits may be stored in an airtight container for up to two days.
Variation: Use orange rind in place of lemon rind, if preferred.
Hints: These biscuits have a chewy texture. They are perfect served with coffee or as an accompaniment with a special ice-cream or mousse for dessert.
Amaretti biscuits may be crumbled over stewed fruit or used whole as a base for trifle.

1

2

3

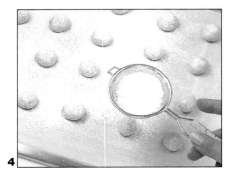
4

AFGHAN BISCUITS

Preparation time: 15 minutes
Total cooking time: 20 minutes
Makes 25

150 g unsalted butter
1/3 cup soft brown sugar
1 egg, lightly beaten
1 teaspoon vanilla essence
1 cup plain flour
2 tablespoons cocoa
    powder
1/3 cup desiccated coconut
1 1/2 cups lightly crushed
    cornflakes
1/2 cup (100 g) choc dots

➤ PREHEAT OVEN to moderate 180°C. Line a 32 x 28 cm biscuit tray with baking paper.

1 Using electric beaters, beat butter and sugar in small mixing bowl until light and creamy. Add egg and essence, beat thoroughly. Transfer mixture to large mixing bowl; add sifted flour and cocoa, coconut and cornflakes. Using a metal spoon, stir until ingredients are just combined and the mixture is almost smooth.

2 Drop one level tablespoon of mixture at a time onto prepared tray. Bake 20 minutes or until lightly browned. Allow biscuits to cool on tray.

3 Place choc dots into small heat-proof bowl. Stand over pan of simmering water and stir until chocolate has melted and mixture is smooth. Remove from heat. Dip tops of biscuits into chocolate; allow to set.

COOK'S FILE

Storage time: Biscuits may be stored in an airtight container for up to two days.

Hint: Sprinkle biscuits with toasted shredded coconut or finely chopped walnuts or pecans.

Variation: Dark chopped chocolate or choc bits can be used instead of choc dots.

1

3

2

PEPPERMINT SLICE

Preparation time: 45 minutes
Total cooking time: 30 minutes
Makes 24

2/3 cup self-raising flour
1/2 cup plain flour
1/4 cup cocoa powder
1/2 cup caster sugar
1 egg, lightly beaten
125 g unsalted butter,
   melted

Mint
1/4 cup cream
2 teaspoons vegetable oil
1 tablespoon liquid glucose
2 cups icing sugar, sifted
peppermint essence

Icing
100 g dark chocolate,
   chopped
1 tablespoon cream
40 g unsalted butter

➤ PREHEAT OVEN to moderate 180°C. Line base and sides of shallow 27 x 18 cm rectangular tin with foil.
1 Sift flours with remaining dry ingredients into medium mixing bowl. Make a well in the centre. Pour combined egg and butter onto dry ingredients. Using a wooden spoon, stir until well combined. Press mixture evenly into the base of prepared tin with hand. Bake 15–20 minutes or until skewer comes out clean when inserted in centre of slice. Cool in tin.
2 **To make Mint:** Combine cream, oil, glucose and icing sugar in medi-um heavy-based pan. Stir over low heat until mixture is smooth and creamy. Add a few drops peppermint essence; mix well. Remove from heat. Pour mixture onto slice base. Smooth with flat-bladed knife. Allow to set.
3 **To make Icing:** Combine chocolate, cream and butter in small heavy-based pan. Stir over low heat until chocolate has melted and mixture is smooth. Spread mixture evenly over mint layer. Refrigerate 5–10 minutes or until set. Remove slice from tin. Cut into 24 even-size squares.

COOK'S FILE

Storage time: Slice can be made up to two days ahead. Store in an air-tight container in a cool, dry place.
Hint: Drizzle with melted white chocolate to decorate if desired.

1

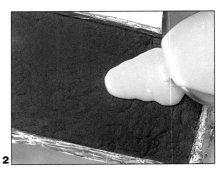

2

3

ANZAC BISCUITS

Preparation time: 12 minutes
Total cooking time: 20 minutes
Makes 26

1 cup plain flour
²/3 cup sugar
1 cup rolled oats
1 cup desiccated coconut
125 g unsalted butter
¼ cup golden syrup
½ teaspoon bicarbonate
 of soda
1 tablespoon boiling water

➤ PREHEAT OVEN to moderate 180°C. Line a 32 x 28 cm biscuit tray with baking paper.

1 Sift flour and sugar into large mixing bowl. Add oats and coconut; make a well in the centre.

2 Combine butter and golden syrup in small pan. Stir over low heat until butter has melted and mixture is smooth; remove from heat. Dissolve soda in water; add immediately to butter mixture. It will foam up instantly. Add butter mixture to dry ingredients. Using a wooden spoon, stir until well combined.

3 Drop one level tablespoon of mix-ture at a time onto prepared tray. Flatten gently with fingers, allowing room for spreading. Bake 20 minutes or until just browned.

4 Remove from oven; transfer to wire rack to cool.

COOK'S FILE

Storage time: Store biscuits in an airtight container for up to three days.
Variation: Use treacle or honey in place of the golden syrup.
Hint: Instant or 1-minute oats are quite suitable for this recipe.

FLAKED ALMOND TUILES

Preparation time: 8 minutes +
  2 hours standing
Total cooking time: 5 minutes each tray
Makes 22

2/3 **cup plain flour**
1/2 **cup caster sugar**
60 g **unsalted butter, melted**
2 **egg whites, lightly beaten**
1/4 **teaspoon almond**
  essence
1/2 **cup toasted flaked**
  almonds

➤ BRUSH TWO 32 x 28 cm biscuit trays with melted butter or oil, line base with paper; grease paper.

1 Sift flour into medium mixing bowl; add sugar. Make a well in the centre. Add butter, egg whites and essence to bowl. Using a wooden spoon, stir until well combined. Cover mixture with plastic wrap; allow to rest for 2 hours.

2 Heat oven to moderate 180°C. Drop 2 level teaspoons of mixture at a time onto prepared trays. Spread mixture to a round 10–12 cm in diameter. Sprinkle each round with flaked almonds.

3 Bake biscuits 5 minutes or until lightly golden. Remove from oven; stand on tray 30 seconds. Carefully loosen and lift biscuits from tray and shape over a bottle or rolling pin.

COOK'S FILE

Storage time: Store biscuits in an airtight container for up to two days.
Hint: It is best to cook only three to four biscuits at a time to allow sufficient time to remove cooked biscuits from tray and mould to shape before cooling. Biscuits will crispen on standing. Tuiles are delicious served with creamy desserts.

MELTING MOMENTS

Preparation time: 15 minutes
Total cooking time: 15 minutes
Makes 45

180 g unsalted butter
¹/3 cup icing sugar
1 teaspoon vanilla essence
¹/3 cup cornflour
1 cup plain flour
100 g packet glacé cherries

➤ PREHEAT OVEN to moderate 180°C. Line a 32 x 28 cm biscuit tray with baking paper.

1 Using electric beaters, beat butter, sugar and essence in small mixing bowl until light and creamy. Using a flat-bladed knife, stir in sifted flours. Stir until just combined and mixture is smooth.

2 Spoon mixture into a piping bag fitted with a 1 cm-wide fluted piping nozzle; pipe mixture into rosettes 4 cm in diameter onto prepared tray.

3 Top each rosette with half a cherry. Bake 15 minutes or until lightly golden and crisp. Transfer biscuits to wire rack to cool.

COOK'S FILE

Storage time: Store biscuits in an airtight container for up to two days.
Variation: Replace glacé cherries with pieces of glacé ginger if desired.
Hint: Sandwich together two Melting Moments with raspberry jam and sift icing sugar over the top.

1

2

3

FLORENTINES

Preparation time: 25 minutes
Total cooking time: 7 minutes each
  batch
Makes 24

1/4 **cup plain flour**
2 **tablespoons chopped walnuts**
2 **tablespoons chopped flaked**
  almonds
2 **tablespoons finely chopped**
  glacé cherries
2 **tablespoons finely chopped**
  mixed peel
75 **g unsalted butter**
1/4 **cup soft brown sugar**
180 **g dark compound**
  chocolate, chopped

➤ PREHEAT OVEN to moderate 180°C. Line a 32 x 28 cm biscuit tray with baking paper.

1 Sift flour into a medium mixing bowl. Add walnuts, almonds, cherries and mixed peel. Stir to combine and make a well in the centre. Combine butter and sugar in a small pan. Stir over a low heat until butter has melted and sugar has dissolved; remove from heat.

2 Add butter mixture to dry ingredients. Using a wooden spoon, stir until just combined; do not over-beat. Drop heaped teaspoons of mixture onto prepared trays, leaving about 7 cm between each one. Press into neat 5 cm rounds. Bake for 7 minutes. Remove tray from oven. While still soft, use a flat-bladed

knife to push biscuits into neat rounds. Cool on tray for 5 minutes before transferring to a wire rack and allowing to cool thoroughly.

3 Place chocolate in a heatproof bowl. Stand over simmering water and stir until chocolate is melted and smooth. Using a flat-bladed knife, carefully spread chocolate on the underside of Florentines. Place biscuits chocolate-side up on a wire rack to set.

COOK'S FILE

Storage time: Florentines are best made on day of serving.
Variation: Try white chocolate melts instead of dark chocolate.
Hint: Florentines are perfect to serve with after-dinner coffee.

COCONUT JAM SLICE

Preparation time: 20 minutes
Total cooking time: 35 minutes
Makes 25 squares

1 1/2 **cups plain flour**
150 **g unsalted butter**
1/2 **cup icing sugar**

Topping
1/3 **cup caster sugar**
2 **eggs**
2 **cups desiccated coconut**
1/3 **cup blackberry jam**

➤ PREHEAT OVEN to moderate 180°C. Brush a 23 cm square cake tin with melted butter or oil. Line base and sides with baking paper, extending over two sides.

1 Place flour, butter and sugar into food processor bowl. Using the pulse action, press button for 30 seconds or until mixture forms a dough. Turn onto a lightly floured surface and knead 20 seconds or until smooth. Press dough into prepared tin; refrigerate 10 minutes. Bake 15 minutes or until just golden; cool.

2 To make Topping: Place

sugar and eggs in a medium mixing bowl and whisk until combined. Stir in coconut.

3 Spread jam over cooled base. Spread topping over jam, pressing down with back of spoon, and bake 20 minutes, until light golden. Cut into 25 squares when cool.

COOK'S FILE

Storage time: Slice may be stored for up to three days in an airtight container.
Variation: Use different flavours of jam, such as boysenberry, raspberry or strawberry, for a change.

Florentines (top) and
Coconut Jam Slice.

GINGERNUT BISCUITS

Preparation time: 15 minutes
Total cooking time: 15 minutes
Makes 55

2 cups plain flour
1/2 teaspoon bicarbonate
    of soda
1 tablespoon ground ginger
1/2 teaspoon mixed spice
125 g unsalted butter
1 cup soft brown sugar
1/4 cup boiling water
1 tablespoon golden syrup

➤ PREHEAT OVEN to moderate 180°C. Line two 32 x 28 cm biscuit trays with baking paper.

1 Sift flour with remaining dry ingredients into large mixing bowl; add chopped butter and sugar. Using fingertips, rub butter into flour for 3 minutes or until mixture is fine and crumbly.

2 Place boiling water in a small jug, add golden syrup and stir until dissolved. Add to flour mixture and mix to a soft dough.

3 Roll 2 teaspoonsful of mixture into balls, place on prepared trays and flatten out slightly with fingertips.

Bake for 15 minutes. Cool on trays for 10 minutes before transferring to a wire rack.

COOK'S FILE

Storage time: Biscuits will keep up to one week in an airtight container.
Variation: Add one tablespoon of chopped glacé ginger for extra flavour.
Hint: To dress biscuits up, combine two to three teaspoons lemon juice, half cup sifted icing sugar and 10 g melted butter, in small bowl. Mix until smooth. Spread over top of biscuits and allow to set.

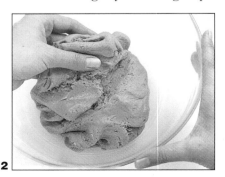

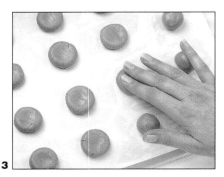

APPLE CRUMBLE SLICE

Preparation time: 20 minutes
Total cooking time: 40 minutes
Makes 24 squares

³/4 **cup self-raising flour**
³/4 **cup plain flour**
1 **cup desiccated coconut**
150 g **unsalted butter**
³/4 **cup soft brown sugar**
410 g **can pie apple**
¹/3 **cup rolled oats**
¹/4 **cup currants**
¹/4 **teaspoon ground cinnamon**

➤ PREHEAT OVEN to moderate 180°C. Brush an 18 x 27 cm shallow rectangular tin with melted butter or oil. Line base and sides with baking paper, extending over two sides.

1 Sift flours into a large mixing bowl; add coconut. Combine butter and sugar in a small pan. Stir over low heat until butter has melted and sugar has dissolved; remove from heat. Pour butter mixture on dry ingredients. Using a wooden spoon, stir until well combined.

2 Reserve one cup of mixture. Press the remaining mixture into prepared tin, smoothing surface with the back of a spoon. Bake for 10 minutes; allow to cool completely.

3 Spread pie apple over cooled base. Combine reserved mixture with oats and currants. Using fingertips, crumble mixture and sprinkle over apple. Dust with cinnamon. Bake for 30 minutes or until top is golden. Cool, lift from tin and cut into squares.

COOK'S FILE

Storage time: Store up to two days in an airtight container.
Variation: Use pie apricots instead of apple.

1

2

3

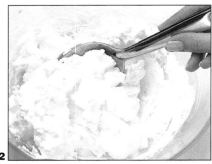

CATS' TONGUES

Preparation time: 12 minutes
Total cooking time: 10 minutes
Makes 40

80 g unsalted butter, chopped
²/3 cup icing sugar, sifted
2 egg whites
2 tablespoons caster sugar
³/4 cup plain flour

➤ PREHEAT OVEN to moderate 180°C. Brush a 32 x 28 cm biscuit tray with melted butter or oil and line base with paper; grease paper.

1 Using electric beaters, beat butter and icing sugar in small bowl until light and creamy. Transfer mixture to large mixing bowl.

2 Place egg whites in small mixing bowl. Using electric beaters, beat egg whites until firm peaks form. Add sugar gradually, beating until mixture is thick and glossy and all sugar is dissolved. Using a metal spoon, fold egg mixture into butter mixture; add sifted flour. Fold flour in quickly and lightly; do not overmix.

3 Spoon mixture into a piping bag fitted with a 1 cm-wide plain piping nozzle; pipe mixture into 8 cm lengths onto prepared tray, allowing room for spreading.

4 Bake 10 minutes or until lightly golden. Stand on tray 1 minute before transferring to wire rack to cool. Dust with icing sugar before serving. Serve with ice-cream.

COOK'S FILE

Storage time: Store biscuits in airtight container for up to two days.
Variation: Add half teaspoon finely grated orange or lemon rind to mixture if desired.

FRUIT AND NUT SLICE

Preparation time: 25 minutes
Total cooking time: 45 minutes
Makes 18 fingers

1 cup plain flour
60 g unsalted butter, chopped
1/3 cup caster sugar
1 teaspoon grated lemon rind
2 tablespoons sour cream

Fruit and Nut Topping
1 cup (190 g) finely chopped
   raisins
1/4 cup finely chopped dried
   dates
1/4 cup finely chopped dried
   (plump) figs
2/3 cup (75 g) chopped walnuts

1/4 cup flaked almonds
2 tablespoons lemon juice
1 egg
1/3 cup soft brown sugar
2 tablespoons plain flour

➤ PREHEAT OVEN to moderate
180°C. Brush a shallow 30 x 20 cm
rectangular cake tin with melted butter or oil. Cover base with paper,
extending over two sides; grease
paper.
1 Sift flour into medium mixing
bowl; add butter, sugar and rind.
Using fingertips, rub butter into flour
for 3 minutes or until mixture is fine
and crumbly. Add cream, press
together to form a soft dough.
2 Press mixture into base of prepared tin; smooth surface, prick evenly with a fork. Bake 15 minutes or

until just golden. Remove from oven.
**3 To make Fruit and Nut
Topping:** Combine fruits and nuts
with lemon juice in large mixing
bowl. Using electric beaters, beat
egg and sugar in small bowl 5 minutes or until mixture is thick and
foamy. Transfer egg mixture to
bowl with fruit; add sifted flour. Stir
with a wooden spoon until just combined. Spread base with topping.
Return to oven and bake a further
30 minutes. Remove from oven; cool
in tin. Cut into 18 diagonal fingers
before serving.

COOK'S FILE

Storage time: Store slice in an airtight container for up to two days.
Hint: Use a combination of different
nuts in place of the walnuts.

Family
FAVOURITES

FAMILY-STYLE GINGERBREAD MEN

Preparation time: 30 minutes
Total cooking time: 10 minutes +
  15 minutes refrigeration
Makes 16

125 g unsalted butter
1/3 cup soft dark brown or soft
  brown sugar
1/4 cup golden syrup
1 egg, lightly beaten
2 cups plain flour
1/4 cup self-raising flour
1 tablespoon ground ginger
1 teaspoon bicarbonate of soda
1 tablespoon currants

Icing
1 egg white
1/2 teaspoon lemon juice
1 1/4 cups icing sugar, sifted
assorted food colourings

➤ PREHEAT OVEN to moderate 180°C. Line two or three oven trays with baking paper.
1 Using electric beaters, beat butter, sugar and syrup in small mixing bowl until light and creamy. Add egg gradually, beating thoroughly after each addition. Transfer mixture to large bowl. Sift dry ingredients onto butter mixture. Mix with a knife until just combined. Combine dough with well-floured hand. Turn dough onto well-floured surface and knead 1–2 minutes or until smooth. Line a large chopping board with baking paper. Roll out dough on board to 5 mm thickness. (Flour rolling pin if necessary to prevent sticking.) Refrigerate (on board) for 15 minutes so dough is firm to cut.
2 Cut dough into shapes with a 13 cm gingerbread man cutter. Press remaining dough together and re-roll. Cut out shapes. Place biscuits on prepared trays. Place currants as eyes and noses on gingerbread men. Bake 10 minutes or until lightly browned. Cool biscuits on trays.
3 To make Icing: Place egg whites in small dry mixing bowl. Using electric beaters, beat egg whites until foamy. Add lemon juice and icing sugar gradually. Beat until thick and creamy. Divide icing into several bowls. Tint the mixture with desired food colourings. Spoon mixture into small paper icing bags, seal open ends. Snip tips off piping bags; pipe faces and clothing onto gingerbread men.

COOK'S FILE

Storage time: When icing is completely dry, store in an airtight container in a cool, dry place for up to three days.

BRANDY SNAPS WITH COFFEE LIQUEUR CREAM

Preparation time: 12 minutes
Total cooking time: 6 minutes
each tray
Makes 25

60 g unsalted butter
2 tablespoons golden syrup
1/3 cup soft brown sugar, lightly
packed
1/4 cup plain flour
11/2 teaspoons ground ginger
80 g dark chocolate, melted

Coffee Liqueur Cream
2/3 cup cream
1 tablespoon icing sugar,
sifted
1 teaspoon instant coffee
granules
1 tablespoon coffee liqueur

➤ PREHEAT OVEN to moderate
180°C. Line two 32 x 28 cm biscuit
trays with baking paper.
1 Combine butter, syrup and sugar
in a small pan. Stir over low heat
until butter has melted and sugar has
dissolved; remove from heat. Add
sifted flour and ginger to pan. Using
a wooden spoon, stir until well combined; do not overbeat.
2 Drop 1 level teaspoon of mixture
at a time onto prepared trays about

12 cm apart. (Prepare only three or
four biscuits at a time.) Spread mixture into 8 cm rounds. Bake 6 minutes or until lightly browned.
3 Stand on trays 30 seconds. Lift
biscuits off tray and wrap around the
handle of a wooden spoon while still
hot; leave to cool. Repeat process
with remaining biscuits.
**4 To make Coffee Liqueur
Cream:** Combine all ingredients in
small mixing bowl; stir until just
combined. Cover with plastic wrap;
refrigerate 1 hour. Using electric

beaters, beat until mixture is thick
and forms stiff peaks. Fill biscuits
with Coffee Liqueur Cream and pipe
or drizzle with melted chocolate
before serving.

COOK'S FILE

Storage time: Store in an airtight
container for up for two days or
freeze snaps for up to one month
without filling.
Hint: Spoon cream into small paper
icing bag. Seal open end and snip off
tip. Pipe into brandy snaps.

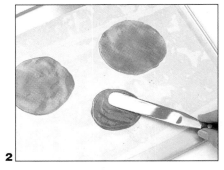

VANILLA CUSTARD KISSES

Preparation time: 15 minutes
Total cooking time: 12 minutes
Makes 40

125 g unsalted butter
1/2 cup caster sugar
2 egg yolks
2 teaspoons vanilla
   essence
1/3 cup custard
   powder
3/4 cup plain flour
3/4 cup self-raising flour

Vanilla Cream
40 g unsalted butter,
   softened
2/3 cup icing sugar, sifted
1 teaspoon vanilla
   essence
1 tablespoon milk

➤ PREHEAT OVEN to moderate 180°C. Brush two 32 x 28 cm biscuit trays with melted butter or oil. Line base with paper; grease paper.

1 Using electric beaters, beat butter and sugar in a small mixing bowl until mixture is light and creamy. Add the egg yolks one at a time, beating thoroughly after each addition. Add vanilla essence; beat until combined.

2 Transfer mixture to large mixing bowl. Using a metal spoon, fold in sifted custard powder and flours. Stir until ingredients are just combined and the mixture is almost smooth. Press mixture together with fingertips to form a soft dough.

3 Roll 1 level teaspoon of mixture at a time into balls. Arrange on prepared trays about 5 cm apart. Flatten lightly with base of a glass to 2.5 cm rounds. Bake 12 minutes or until biscuits are golden.

4 To make Vanilla Cream: Beat butter and essence in small bowl with a wooden spoon until smooth. Add sugar and milk gradually; stir until well combined and mixture is smooth. Stand biscuits on trays 5 minutes; transfer to a wire rack to cool. Spread half the biscuits with filling and sandwich together with remaining biscuits.

COOK'S FILE

Storage time: Store biscuits in airtight container for up to two days.
Hint: Dust biscuits with sifted icing sugar to serve.

CORNFLAKE COOKIES

Preparation time: 12 minutes
Total cooking time: 20 minutes
Makes 30

125 g unsalted butter
3/4 cup sugar
2 eggs, lightly beaten
1 teaspoon vanilla essence
2 tablespoons currants
1 1/2 cups desiccated coconut
1/2 teaspoon bicarbonate of
    soda
1/2 teaspoon baking
    powder
2 cups plain flour
3 cups cornflakes, lightly
    crushed

➤ PREHEAT OVEN to moderate 180°C. Line a 32 x 28 cm biscuit tray with baking paper.

1 Using electric beaters, beat butter and sugar in small mixing bowl until light and creamy. Add eggs gradually, beating thoroughly after each addition. Add essence; beat until combined.

2 Transfer mixture to a large mixing bowl; add currants and coconut. Using a metal spoon, fold in sifted soda, powder and flour. Stir until ingredients are just combined and the mixture is almost smooth. Drop level tablespoons of mixture onto the cornflakes; roll into balls. Arrange on prepared tray, allowing room for spreading.

3 Bake 20 minutes or until crisp and golden. Transfer biscuits to wire rack to cool. Store in airtight container.

COOK'S FILE

Storage time: Cookies may be stored for up to three days in an airtight container.

Variation: Roll mixture in crushed Rice Bubbles if preferred.

COCONUT MACAROONS

Preparation time: 15 minutes
Total cooking time: 15–20 minutes
Makes 60

3 egg whites
1 1/4 cups caster sugar
1/2 teaspoon coconut essence
1 teaspoon grated lemon rind
2 tablespoons cornflour, sifted
3 cups desiccated coconut
125 g dark chocolate melts,
     melted

➤ PREHEAT OVEN to moderately slow 160°C. Line two 32 x 28 cm biscuit trays with baking paper.

1 Place egg whites in a small, dry mixing bowl. Using electric beaters, beat egg whites until firm peaks form. Add sugar gradually, beating constantly until mixture is thick and glossy and all the sugar is dissolved. Add essence and rind; beat until just combined.

2 Transfer mixture to large mixing bowl; add cornflour and coconut. Using a metal spoon, stir until just combined.

3 Drop 2 level teaspoons of mixture onto prepared trays about 3 cm apart. Bake on top shelf 15–20 minutes or until golden.

4 Cool macaroons on trays. Dip half of each biscuit into melted chocolate; allow to set before serving.

COOK'S FILE

Storage time: Store in an airtight container for up to two days.
Hint: Sprinkle biscuits with shredded coconut before baking. Drizzle with melted chocolate, instead of dipping, for decoration.

COFFEE HAZELNUT BISCUITS

Preparation time: 15 minutes,
    plus 30 minutes in freezer
Total cooking time: 15 minutes
Makes 25

1¼ cups plain flour
100 g unsalted butter, chopped
⅓ cup caster sugar
3 teaspoons instant coffee
    granules
2 teaspoons boiling water
1 egg yolk
⅓ cup ground hazelnuts
⅔ cup finely chopped
    hazelnuts
13 whole hazelnuts, halved

Coffee Glacé Icing
½ cup pure icing sugar
½ teaspoon instant coffee
10 g butter, softened
2 teaspoons milk

➤ BRUSH TWO 32 x 28 cm biscuit trays with melted butter or oil. Line base with paper; grease paper.

1 Sift flour into large mixing bowl; add butter and sugar. Using your fingertips, rub butter into the flour for 2 minutes or until mixture is fine and crumbly. Make a well in the centre.

2 Dissolve coffee in water. Add egg, cooled coffee and ground hazelnuts to bowl. Mix with fingers until mixture is soft and almost smooth.

3 Turn dough onto lightly floured surface. Knead for 1 minute or until smooth; shape dough into a 30 cm-long x 4 cm-wide log. Roll log in chopped hazelnuts. Cover, and place in freezer for 30 minutes. Heat oven to moderate 180°C. Using a sharp knife, cut log evenly into 25 slices. Place on prepared trays about 3 cm apart. Bake 15 minutes or until golden. Cool on trays.

To make Icing: Sift icing sugar into bowl; stir in coffee, butter and milk. Stand bowl over warm water; mix until smooth. Spread little in centre of each biscuit; top with a half hazelnut.

COOK'S FILE

Storage time: Store biscuits in airtight container for up to three days.
Variation: Use walnuts or pecans to replace the hazelnuts.

CHOCOLATE CARAMEL SLICE

Preparation time: 15 minutes
Total cooking time: 20 minutes
Makes 24 triangles

125 g plain sweet biscuits, crushed
80 g unsalted butter, melted
2 tablespoons desiccated coconut
400 g can sweetened condensed milk
125 g butter
1/3 cup caster sugar
1/3 cup golden syrup
250 g milk chocolate melts
1 tablespoon vegetable oil

➤ Brush a shallow 30 x 20 cm rectangular cake tin with melted butter or oil. Line base and sides with aluminium foil; grease foil.

1 Combine biscuits, melted butter and coconut together in a medium mixing bowl. Press mixture evenly into prepared pan; smooth surface.

2 Combine condensed milk, butter, sugar and syrup in small pan. Stir over low heat 15 minutes or until sugar has dissolved and mixture is smooth and thick. Remove from heat; cool slightly. Pour over biscuit base; smooth surface.

3 Place milk chocolate melts and oil in small heatproof bowl. Stand over pan of simmering water, stir until melted and mixture is smooth. Spread chocolate mixture over caramel. Allow to partially set before marking into 24 triangles. Refrigerate until firm.

COOK'S FILE

Storage time: Slice may be stored in an airtight container for up to two days.
Variation: Use dark chocolate melts in place of milk chocolate.

WALNUT BROWNIES

Preparation time: 10 minutes
Total cooking time: 35 minutes
Makes 20 diamonds

100 g unsalted butter
2/3 cup soft brown sugar
3/4 cup water
1/4 cup sultanas, chopped
1 cup self-raising flour
1 cup plain flour
1 teaspoon ground cinnamon
1 tablespoon cocoa powder
1/2 cup (75 g) chopped walnuts
1/4 cup choc bits
20 walnut halves

Icing
60 g unsalted butter
3/4 cup icing sugar
1 tablespoon cocoa powder
1 tablespoon milk

➤ PREHEAT OVEN to moderate 180°C. Brush shallow 27 x 18 cm rectangular tin with oil. Cover base with baking paper, extending it over the two longer sides; grease paper.

1 Combine butter, sugar, water and sultanas in small pan. Stir over low heat for 5 minutes until butter is melted and sugar is dissolved; remove from heat.

2 Sift dry ingredients into large mixing bowl; add nuts and choc bits. Make a well in centre. Add butter mixture to dry ingredients. Using a wooden spoon, stir until just combined; do not overbeat.

3 Spoon mixture evenly in prepared tin; smooth surface. Bake 30 minutes

or until skewer comes out clean when inserted in centre of slice.

4 Leave slice in tin 20 minutes before turning onto wire rack to cool. **To make Icing:** Beat butter until light and creamy; add sugar, cocoa and milk. Beat until smooth. Spread over brownie. Cut into diamonds; top each with a walnut.

COOK'S FILE

Storage time: Brownies may be stored in an airtight container for up to three days.

CRUNCHY MUESLI SLICE

Preparation time: 10 minutes
Total cooking time: 50 minutes
Makes 18 fingers

250 g unsalted butter
1 cup caster sugar
2 tablespoons honey
2¼ cups rolled oats
¾ cup desiccated coconut
1 cup cornflakes, lightly
    crushed
⅓ cup flaked almonds
1 teaspoon mixed spice

½ cup finely chopped dried
    apricots
1 cup mixed dried fruit

➤ PREHEAT OVEN to moderately slow 160°C. Brush a shallow 30 x 20 cm rectangular cake tin with melted butter or oil. Line base and sides with paper; grease paper.

1 Combine butter, sugar and honey in small pan. Stir over low heat 5 minutes or until butter has melted and sugar has dissolved. Remove from heat.

2 Place oats, coconut, cornflakes, almonds, spice and fruit in large mixing bowl; stir. Make a well in centre. Pour butter and sugar mixture onto dry ingredients; combine thoroughly.

3 Press mixture firmly into prepared pan. Using a sharp knife, score slice into 18 fingers. (Do not cut through to base). Bake 45 minutes or until golden. Stand in pan 15 minutes before turning out onto a board to cool. Cut into fingers when cool.

COOK'S FILE

Storage time: Store in an airtight container for up to three days.
Variation: Golden syrup may be used instead of honey.

1

2

3

APPLE AND DATE SLICE

Preparation time: 15 minutes +
 30 minutes in freezer
Total cooking time: 45 minutes
Makes: 20 fingers

½ cup wholemeal plain flour
½ cup self-raising flour
½ teaspoon mixed spice
125 g unsalted butter,
 chopped
1 cup rolled oats
2 tablespoons honey
1 egg yolk

Filling
1½ cups (250 g) finely
 chopped dried dates

2 teaspoons grated orange rind
⅓ cup orange juice
2 tablespoons honey, extra
1 cup (375 g) canned pie apple

➤ BRUSH a shallow 30 x 20 cm rectangular cake tin with melted butter or oil. Cover base with paper extending over two sides; grease paper.

1 Sift flours and spice into large mixing bowl; add butter. Using fingertips, rub butter into flour for 3 minutes or until mixture is fine and crumbly. Add oats; stir. Make a well in centre; add honey and yolk and mix with fingers until ingredients are just combined and mixture is soft.

2 Press two-thirds of mixture into base of prepared tin; smooth surface. Shape remaining mixture into a ball,

cover with plastic wrap; freeze 30 minutes.

3 To make Filling: Combine dates, rind, juice and honey in small pan. Stir over low heat 5 minutes without boiling or until thick. Remove from heat, stir in apple; cool. Preheat oven to moderate 180°C. Spread cooled filling evenly over base. Coarsely grate frozen dough evenly over filling. Bake 30 minutes or until lightly browned. Cool in tray. Cut into 20 fingers before serving.

COOK'S FILE

Storage time: Slice may be stored in an airtight container for up to two days.
Variation: Replace dates with prunes or raisins, if preferred.

JUMBO CHOCOLATE CHIP COOKIES

Preparation time: 20 minutes
Total cooking time: 12 minutes
Makes 25

1½ cups plain flour
¾ cup cocoa powder
1½ cups soft brown sugar
180 g unsalted butter
150 g dark chocolate,
 chopped
3 eggs, lightly beaten
1½ cups choc bits

➤ PREHEAT OVEN to moderate 180°C. Line two 32 x 28 cm biscuit trays with baking paper.

1 Sift flour and cocoa into a large mixing bowl; add sugar. Make a well in the centre.

2 Combine butter and chocolate in a small pan. Stir over a low heat until mixture is melted and smooth; remove from heat.

3 Add butter mixture and eggs to dry ingredients. Using a wooden spoon, stir until well combined; do not overbeat. Stir in choc bits. Drop 2 level tablespoons of mixture onto prepared trays, allowing room for

spreading. Flatten each one slightly with fingertips. Bake for 12 minutes. Cool on trays for 5 minutes before transferring to a wire rack to cool.

COOK'S FILE

Storage time: Cookies may be stored for up to two days in an airtight container.
Variation: For a more sophisticated version, half or all the choc bits could be replaced with roughly chopped macadamia nuts.
Hint: The size of biscuits can be varied; one tablespoon instead of two will make an average-size cookie.

*Apple and Date Slice (top)
and Jumbo Chocolate Chip Cookies.*

CHOCOLATE HEDGEHOG SLICE

Preparation time: 30 minutes
Total cooking time: 5–10 minutes +
  refrigeration
Makes 50

250 g chocolate cream biscuits,
  finely crushed
1/2 cup desiccated coconut
1 cup pecans, roughly chopped
1 tablespoon cocoa powder,
  sifted
100 g dark chocolate, chopped
80 g unsalted butter
1 tablespoon golden syrup
1 egg, lightly beaten

extra pecans, for decoration
60 g dark chocolate melts, extra

Icing
100 g dark chocolate, chopped
40 g unsalted butter

➤ LINE BASE and sides of shallow
30 x 20 cm rectangular tin with foil.
1 Combine biscuit crumbs, coconut,
pecans and cocoa in medium mixing
bowl. Make a well in the centre.
2 Combine chocolate, butter and
syrup in small heavy-based pan. Stir
over low heat until chocolate and
butter have melted and mixture is
smooth. Remove from heat. Pour
combined chocolate mixture and egg
onto dry ingredients. Using a wooden

spoon, stir until well combined. Press
mixture evenly into prepared tin.
Refrigerate 30 minutes or until set.
3 To make Icing: Place chocolate
and butter in small heatproof bowl.
Stand over pan of simmering water.
Stir until chocolate and butter have
melted and mixture is smooth. Cool
slightly. Spread mixture evenly over
slice base. Refrigerate until set.
Remove slice from tin. Cut into small
squares with sharp knife. Decorate
squares with pecans dipped in extra
melted chocolate.

COOK'S FILE

Storage time: Store slice in airtight
container in the refrigerator for up to
one week.

1

2

3

VANILLA PASSIONFRUIT SLICE

Preparation time: 35 minutes
Total cooking time: 20-25 minutes
Makes 12

2 sheets ready-rolled puff pastry

Custard
1/4 cup custard powder
1/4 cup caster sugar
1 cup cream
1 1/2 cups milk
1/2 teaspoon vanilla essence

Icing
1/4 cup passionfruit pulp
25 g unsalted butter
1 1/2 cups icing sugar

➤ PREHEAT OVEN to moderately hot 210°C (190°C gas). Line two oven trays with baking paper.

1 Place pastry sheets on prepared trays and prick all over with a fork. Bake 10–15 minutes or until golden and crisp. Cool on wire rack.

2 To make Custard: Blend custard powder, sugar and cream in medium heavy-based pan. Gradually stir in milk and stir constantly over medium heat until custard boils and thickens. Remove from heat. Stir in essence. Place plastic wrap onto the surface of custard to prevent a skin forming. Cool completely.

3 Place one sheet of pastry onto a board. Spread custard evenly over surface. Top with remaining pastry sheet upside down.

4 To make Icing: Combine pulp, butter and icing sugar in medium heatproof bowl. Stand over pan of simmering water and stir until icing is smooth and glossy; remove from heat. Spread icing evenly over pastry sheet, using a flat-bladed knife. Refrigerate several hours or until pastry softens slightly. Cut slice into squares using a serrated knife.

COOK'S FILE

Storage time: Pastry can be prepared one day in advance. Store in an airtight container. Store assembled slice in an airtight container in the refrigerator for up to two days.
Hint: Use fresh or canned passionfruit pulp in the icing.

1

2

3

4

FAMILY-STYLE ROCKY ROAD SLICE

Preparation time: 35 minutes
Total cooking time: 20-30 minutes
Makes 2 slices

150 g unsalted butter
1/3 cup icing sugar, sifted
1 1/4 cups self-raising flour
2 tablespoons cocoa powder
250 g coloured marshmallows
100 g coloured glacé cherries,
    halved
200 g dark chocolate, chopped
15 g white vegetable shortening

➤ PREHEAT OVEN to moderately slow 160°C. Brush two 26 x 8 x 4.5 cm bar tins with melted butter or oil. Line with baking paper.

1 Using electric beaters, beat butter and sugar until light and creamy; transfer to large bowl. Using a metal spoon, fold in combined sifted flour and cocoa; mix well. Divide mixture evenly between both tins. Press mixture into tin using fingertips. Bake 20–25 minutes or until lightly coloured. Stand in tins to cool.

2 Top bases randomly with marshmallows and cherries.

3 Place chocolate and shortening in medium heatproof bowl. Stand over pan of simmering water and stir until chocolate and shortening have melted and mixture is smooth. Cool slightly.

4 Spoon chocolate mixture evenly over both slices. Tap tins gently on bench to distribute chocolate evenly. Allow chocolate to set. Cut slice into squares or fingers.

COOK'S FILE

Storage time: Slice may be stored in an airtight container, in a cool dry place, for up to four days.

Variation: In each tin, sprinkle 1/4 cup of roughly chopped mixed nuts over the marshmallows and cherries before spooning on the chocolate topping.

Hint: If the weather is hot, and it is necessary to refrigerate slice to set the chocolate, allow it to come to room temperature before cutting into pieces.

MONTE CREAMS

Preparation time: 30 minutes
Total cooking time: 15–20 minutes
Makes 25

125 g unsalted butter
1/2 cup caster sugar
1/4 cup milk
11/2 cups self-raising flour, sifted
1/4 cup custard powder, sifted
1/3 cup desiccated coconut

Filling
75 g unsalted butter
2/3 cup icing sugar

2 teaspoons milk
1/3 cup strawberry jam

➤ PREHEAT OVEN to 180°C. Line two 32 x 28 cm biscuit trays with baking paper.

1 Using electric beaters, beat butter and sugar in a medium mixing bowl until light and creamy. Add milk, beat until combined. Add flour, custard powder and coconut and mix to form a soft dough.

2 Roll two teaspoonsful of mixture into balls. Place on prepared trays. Press with a fork. Dip fork in custard powder occasionally to prevent sticking. Bake for 15–20 minutes, until

just golden. Transfer to a wire rack to cool completely before filling.

3 To make Filling: Using electric beaters, beat butter and icing sugar until light and creamy. Add milk and beat until combined. Spread one biscuit with about half teaspoon of butter mixture, and one with about half teaspoon of jam; sandwich together.

COOK'S FILE

Storage time: Biscuits may be stored up to four days in an airtight container.

Variation: Use apricot jam in place of the strawberry.

1

2

3

JAM DROPS

Preparation time: 20 minutes
Total cooking time: 15 minutes
Makes 32

80 g unsalted butter
1/3 cup caster sugar
2 tablespoons milk
1/2 teaspoon vanilla
  essence
1 cup self-raising flour

1/3 cup custard powder
2 tablespoons raspberry jam

➤ PREHEAT OVEN to moderate 180°C. Line two 32 x 28 cm biscuit trays with baking paper.
1 Using electric beaters, beat butter and sugar in a small mixing bowl until light and creamy. Add milk and essence; beat until combined.
2 Add sifted flour and custard powder and mix to form a soft dough. Roll two teaspoonsful of mixture into

balls and place on prepared tray.
3 Make an indentation in each ball using the end of a wooden spoon. Fill each hole with quarter teaspoon jam. Bake for 15 minutes, transfer to a wire rack to cool.

COOK'S FILE

Storage time: Biscuits may be stored for up to five days in an airtight container.
Hint: Dust with sifted icing sugar just before serving.

ORANGE POPPYSEED COOKIES

Preparation time: 30 minutes
Total cooking time: 15 minutes
Makes 60

75 g unsalted butter
3/4 cup caster sugar
1 egg
1 1/2 teaspoons finely grated orange rind
2 teaspoons orange juice
1 1/4 cups plain flour
1/4 cup cornflour
1/4 teaspoon bicarbonate of soda
1 tablespoon buttermilk
2 tablespoons poppyseeds
185 g white chocolate melts

➤ PREHEAT OVEN to 180°C. Line two 32 x 28 cm biscuit trays with baking paper.

1 Using electric beaters, beat butter, sugar and egg in a small bowl until light and creamy. Add the orange rind and juice and beat until combined. Transfer the mixture to a medium bowl.

2 Add sifted flour, cornflour, bicarbonate of soda, buttermilk and poppyseeds; mix to a soft dough using a flat-bladed knife.

3 Drop mixture, two teaspoonsful at a time, onto the prepared trays. Press a white chocolate melt into the centre of each cookie. Bake for 15 minutes or until just golden. Cool cookies on trays for 5 minutes before transferring to a wire rack to cool.

COOK'S FILE

Storage time: Cookies may be stored up to three days in an airtight container.
Hint: Top with an orange glacé icing if desired.

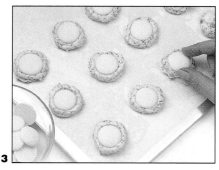

Scrumptious SHORTBREAD

FRUITY SHORTBREAD PILLOWS

Preparation time: 1 hour
Total cooking time: 15–20 minutes
Makes 18

2 cups plain flour
1/2 cup icing sugar
185 g chilled unsalted butter,
  chopped
1 egg
1/4 cup fruit mince
1 egg, extra, lightly beaten

➤ PREHEAT OVEN to moderate 180°C. Line two oven trays with baking paper.

1 Place flour, sugar and butter in food processor bowl. Using the pulse action, press button for 20 seconds or until the mixture is fine and crumbly. Add egg, process for a further 15 seconds or until the mixture comes together. Turn onto a lightly floured surface and knead 2–3 minutes or until dough is smooth. Leave dough, covered with plastic wrap, in refrigerator for 10–15 minutes.

2 Divide pastry in two. Roll half the pastry on a sheet of baking paper to 4 mm thickness. Lightly mark round circles with a 4 cm cutter. Spoon half teaspoon of fruit mince into the cen-

tre of each circle. Brush pastry surface with egg.

3 On a sheet of baking paper, roll remaining pastry to 3 mm thickness. (Pastry should be rolled into a slightly larger circle, approximately 1.5 cm extra in diameter.) Carefully lift pastry, using the rolling pin as a lever, over the top of first pastry sheet. Press down between the filling to seal edges. Cut biscuits, using a floured 4 cm round cutter. The biscuits should look like little pillows. Place on prepared oven trays and bake 15–20 minutes or until pale golden. Cool biscuits on trays. Dust liberally with sifted icing sugar before serving.

COOK'S FILE

Storage time: Biscuits may be stored in an airtight container for up to three days.

Hint: Make the biscuits a different shape by using a square or oval cutter, instead of round.

Variations: Add 1 tablespoon of chopped walnuts to the fruit mince, for a fruit and nut variation. If fruit mince is not available, use 1/4 cup of finely chopped mixed dried fruit, with 2–3 teaspoons of rum or brandy. Mix well and leave to stand 30 minutes or until the fruit has absorbed the liquid. Fruit juice can be used in place of rum or brandy.

GREEK SHORTBREAD

Preparation time: 40 minutes
Total cooking time: 15 minutes
Makes about 38

200 g butter
1 cup icing sugar, sifted
1 teaspoon finely grated
    orange rind
1 egg
1 egg yolk
2¹/₂ cups plain flour
1¹/₂ teaspoons baking powder
1 teaspoon ground cinnamon
250 g blanched almonds,
    toasted, finely chopped
icing sugar, extra

➤ PREHEAT OVEN to moderately slow 160°C. Line an oven tray with baking paper.

1 Using electric beaters, beat butter, sugar and rind in a small mixing bowl until light and creamy. Add egg and egg yolk, beating in thoroughly.

2 Transfer mixture to large mixing bowl. Using a metal spoon, fold in sifted flour, baking powder, cinnamon and almonds; mix until well combined.

3 Shape level tablespoons of mixture into crescent shapes. Place on prepared trays. Bake 15 minutes or until lightly golden. Stand 5 minutes before transferring biscuits to wire rack to cool. While still warm, dust with icing sugar. Just before serving, heavily dust again with icing sugar.

COOK'S FILE

Storage time: Store crescents in airtight container, dusted heavily with icing sugar, for up to a week.

Variation: Roasted hazelnuts may be used instead of almonds.

BASIC SHORTBREAD FINGERS

Preparation time: 8 minutes
Total cooking time: 20 minutes
Makes 20 fingers

¾ cup cornflour
⅓ cup fine ground rice flour
⅔ cup plain flour
⅓ cup icing sugar
200 g unsalted butter, chopped

➤ PREHEAT OVEN to moderate 180°C. Brush a 32 x 28 cm biscuit tray with melted butter or oil, line base with paper; grease paper.

1 Sift flours and sugar into large mixing bowl; add butter. Using fingertips, rub butter into flour for 3 minutes or until mixture is fine and crumbly. Press mixture together with fingers to form a soft dough.

2 Press mixture into a shallow foil-lined 18 x 27 cm rectangular tin; smooth surface. Turn mixture onto a board. Rough up surface with a grater or mark with a fork if desired. Cut into half lengthways, then cut each half into 2 cm strips.

3 Arrange on prepared tray about 3 cm apart; bake 20 minutes or until firm and lightly golden.

COOK'S FILE

Storage time: Biscuits may be stored in an airtight container for up to a week.

Hint: Dust with icing sugar to serve.

1

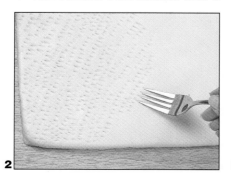

2

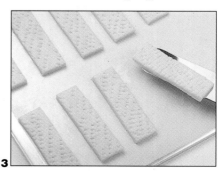

3

MARZIPAN SWIRLS

Preparation time: 10 minutes
Total cooking time: 10 minutes
Makes 30

100 g unsalted butter,
  chopped
100 g purchased marzipan log,
  chopped
2 tablespoons icing sugar
2 egg yolks
1/2 cup self-raising flour
1/2 cup plain flour
coloured cachous

➤ PREHEAT OVEN to moderate 180°C. Line a 32 x 28 cm biscuit tray with baking paper.

1 Using electric beaters, beat butter, marzipan and sugar in small mixing bowl until light and creamy. Add yolk and beat further 1 minute. Transfer to a large mixing bowl.

2 Using a metal spoon, fold in sifted flours. Stir until just combined and mixture is smooth. Spoon mixture into piping bag fitted with a fluted nozzle, 1 cm in diameter.

3 Pipe stars onto trays about 4 cm in diameter, 3 cm apart. Top each star with a cachou. Bake 10 minutes or until lightly golden. Stand biscuits on tray 5 minutes before transferring to wire rack to cool. Dust with icing sugar before serving.

COOK'S FILE

Storage time: Biscuits can be stored in an airtight container for up to a week.

Hint: Marzipan log is available in most supermarkets and some delicatessens. To make marzipan, combine 200 g ground almonds with 1 cup sifted icing sugar. Add a beaten egg white and 1/2 teaspoon liquid glucose and knead together.

CHOCOLATE HAZELNUT WEDGES

Preparation time: 30 minutes
Total cooking time: 50 minutes
Makes 16

150 g unsalted butter
1/2 cup icing sugar
1/3 cup ground hazelnuts
1 1/4 cups plain flour
50 g dark chocolate melts
80 g white chocolate melts

➤ PREHEAT OVEN to slow 150°C. Brush a shallow 21 cm round, fluted flan tin with melted butter or oil.

1 Using electric beaters, beat butter and sugar until light and creamy. Add nuts and beat until combined. Transfer mixture to large mixing bowl. Using a metal spoon, fold in sifted flour. Mix well.

2 Press mixture evenly into prepared tin; smooth surface. Score into 16 wedges, using a sharp knife. Bake 35–40 minutes or until pale golden. Stand in tin to cool.

3 Carefully remove shortbread from tin. Using a sharp knife, cut into scored wedges.

4 Place dark chocolate in a small heatproof bowl. Stand over pan of simmering water and stir until chocolate is melted and smooth. Allow to cool slightly. Spoon chocolate into small paper icing bag, seal open end. Snip off tip. Pipe a wide strip down the centre of each wedge. Melt white chocolate melts in same way as dark chocolate. Pipe a white zigzag pattern over the dark chocolate stripe. Allow to set.

Storage time: Store wedges in an airtight container in a cool, dry place for up to three days.
Variation: Use ground almonds or walnuts in this recipe to replace the hazelnuts.

PASSIONFRUIT SHORTBREAD

Preparation time: 45 minutes
Total cooking time: 20 minutes
Makes about 40

250 g butter
1/3 cup caster sugar
2 1/4 cups plain flour
1/4 cup rice flour
40 g white choc melts, melted

Passionfruit Icing
1 1/4 cups icing sugar, sifted
2 tablespoons passionfruit
    pulp
20 g softened butter
1 tablespoon water

➤ PREHEAT OVEN to moderately slow 160°C. Line two oven trays with baking paper.

1 Using electric beaters, beat butter and sugar in small mixing bowl until light and creamy. Using a metal spoon, fold in sifted flours. Turn dough onto lightly floured surface. Knead gently 1 minute or until smooth.

2 Roll out dough between two sheets of baking paper to 6 mm thickness. Using a sharp knife, cut into 4 x 4 cm diamonds. Place on prepared trays, allowing room for spreading. Reroll remaining pastry and cut out diamonds in the same way. Bake for 15 minutes or until biscuits are lightly brown. Stand for 5 minutes before transferring onto a wire rack to cool.

3 To make Passionfruit Icing: Combine icing sugar, passionfruit pulp, butter and water in bowl to form a smooth paste. Stand bowl in pan of simmering water, stirring until icing is smooth and glossy. Remove the pan from heat; allow icing in bowl to stand in water while icing biscuits. Using a flat-bladed knife, spread the top of each diamond with 1/2 teaspoon of icing.

4 Stand biscuits 15 minutes to set, then drizzle or pipe a decorative pattern on top with melted white chocolate.

COOK'S FILE

Storage time: Biscuits may be stored in an airtight container for up to two days.

Hints: Overheating the icing will make it dull and grainy. Work quickly while icing, and dip the knife into hot water occasionally to give a smooth, shiny finish.

If fresh passionfruit is out of season, substitute canned pulp.

Rice flour is a fine gluten-free flour, made from ground brown or white rice. It is often used to make Chinese noodles. Rice flour may be obtained from supermarkets and health food shops. If rice flour is not available, substitute plain white flour.

1

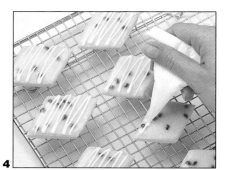

2

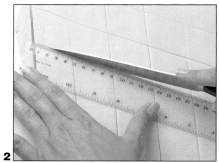

3

4

1

2

3

4

WHOLEMEAL APRICOT SLICE

Preparation time: 25 minutes
Total cooking time: 25 minutes
Makes 24

200 g unsalted butter
1/2 cup caster sugar
1 cup plain flour
1 cup wholemeal self-raising flour

Filling
200 g dried apricots, finely chopped
2 teaspoons honey
3/4 cup water

➤ PREHEAT OVEN to moderate 180°C.

1 Brush a 27 x 18 cm shallow rectangular tin with melted butter or oil. Line tin with baking paper extending over two sides.

2 Using electric beaters, beat butter and sugar until light and creamy. Add sifted plain and wholemeal flours and mix to a soft dough. Place two-thirds of the dough in prepared tin and smooth surface with the back of a metal spoon.

3 To make Filling: Combine apricots, honey and water in a small pan. Stir over medium heat until mixture boils. Reduce heat and simmer for 5 minutes or until liquid has evaporated. Cool.

4 Spread cooled filling onto base. Crumble remaining dough in fingers and sprinkle over filling. Bake for 25 minutes or until golden. Cool and cut into squares.

COOK'S FILE

Storage time: Slice may be stored up to three days in an airtight container.

Variation: Use any dried fruit or combination of different fruits for the filling. Peaches, pears, apples and ginger would all be suitable.

SHORTBREAD STARS WITH LEMON GLAZE

Preparation time: 20 minutes
Total cooking time: 15 minutes
Makes 35

2 cups plain flour
2 tablespoons rice flour
200 g unsalted butter
1/3 cup icing sugar
1 teaspoon finely grated lemon rind
2 tablespoons lemon juice
silver cachous

Lemon Glaze
1 cup pure icing sugar
2 tablespoons lemon juice, strained
yellow or orange food colouring

➤ PREHEAT OVEN to moderate 180°C. Line two 32 x 28 cm biscuit trays with baking paper.

1 Place flours, butter and sugar in food processor bowl. Using pulse action, press button for 30 seconds or until mixture is fine and crumbly. Add rind and juice; process 20 seconds until mixture forms a dough.

2 Turn out onto a lightly floured sur-face and knead 20 seconds or until smooth. Roll out to 7 mm thickness; cut out 6 cm star shapes. Bake 15 minutes. Transfer to wire rack to cool.

3 To make Lemon Glaze: Place icing sugar and lemon juice in heat-proof bowl over pan of hot water; stir until smooth. Dip biscuits face down in glaze, drain excess. Dip toothpick or skewer into food colouring and draw lines into icing before it sets. Decorate centre with silver cachou.

COOK'S FILE

Storage time: Store up to five days in an airtight container.

SCOTTISH SHORTBREAD

Preparation time: 20 minutes
Total cooking time: 40 minutes
Makes 8 wedges

1 cup plain flour
¹/₂ cup rice flour
150 g unsalted butter
¹/₄ cup caster sugar
1 teaspoon caster sugar, extra

➤ PREHEAT OVEN to moderately slow 160°C.

1 Using a bowl as a guide, draw an 18 cm circle on baking paper. Sift flours into a large mixing bowl; add chopped butter and sugar.

2 Using fingertips, rub butter into flour for 5 minutes or until mixture forms a dough. Turn out onto a lightly floured surface; knead 30 seconds or until smooth.

3 Turn paper pencil-side down and press out dough to fit circle. Pinch edges to decorate. Score into eight wedges. Sprinkle with extra caster sugar and bake for 40 minutes. Cool on wire rack and break into scored wedges to serve.

COOK'S FILE

Storage time: Store up to four days in an airtight container.

Hint: Shortbread will come out of the oven soft and firm up when cold.

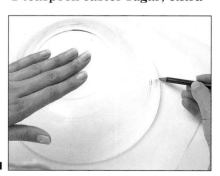

1

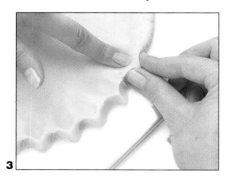

2

3

GINGER SHORTBREAD DREAMS

Preparation time: 25 minutes
Total cooking time: 15 minutes
Makes 22

$^{1}/_{2}$ cup plain flour
$^{1}/_{2}$ cup self-raising flour
2 tablespoons cornflour
100 g unsalted butter, chopped
2 tablespoons soft brown
   sugar

Filling
60 g unsalted butter
$^{1}/_{3}$ cup icing sugar
1 tablespoon finely chopped
   glacé ginger

➤ PREHEAT OVEN to moderate 180°C. Line two 32 x 28 cm biscuit trays with baking paper.
1 Place flours, butter and sugar in food processor bowl. Using the pulse action, press button for 30 seconds or until mixture forms a dough. Turn out onto a lightly floured surface, knead 20 seconds or until smooth.
2 Roll level teaspoonsful of mixture into balls. Place on prepared trays; press with a fork in a criss-cross pattern. Bake for 15 minutes, until just golden. Transfer biscuits to a wire rack to cool completely before filling.
3 To make Filling: Using electric beaters, beat butter and sugar until light and creamy; add ginger and beat until combined. Spread half the biscuits with filling and sandwich with plain ones.

COOK'S FILE

Storage time: Store up to three days in an airtight container.
Variation: Add one teaspoon of ground ginger to biscuit mixture.

1   **2**   **3**

CONTINENTAL FINGERS

Preparation time: 25 minutes
Total cooking time: 15 minutes
Makes 20

200 g unsalted butter
1/4 cup caster sugar
1 teaspoon vanilla
   essence
1 cup plain flour
1/2 cup cornflour
40 g dark chocolate, chopped
40 g white chocolate melts

➤ PREHEAT OVEN to moderate 180°C. Line two 25 x 38 cm biscuit trays with baking paper.

1 Using electric beaters, beat butter and sugar until light and creamy. Add essence and beat until combined. Add the sifted flours and mix to a soft dough.

2 Spoon mixture into a piping bag fitted with a plain 1 cm nozzle. Pipe strips, cutting at pipe end into 8 cm lengths. Bake 15 minutes until just golden. Transfer to wire rack to cool.

3 Place dark chocolate in a small heatproof bowl. Stand over simmering water until chocolate is melted and smooth. Cool slightly. Drizzle or pipe decorative lines across the fingers with the melted chocolate and place on wire rack to set. When dark chocolate is set, repeat with white chocolate melts.

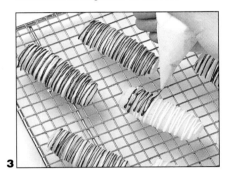

COOK'S FILE

Storage time: Biscuits may be stored up to five days in an airtight container.
Hint: Melts are made of compound chocolate, with fats added to the cocoa, so it sets at room temperature and is easy to work with. Dark chocolate is superior in flavour.

COFFEE PECAN SLICE

Preparation time: 30 minutes
Total cooking time: 40 minutes
Makes 15

1 1/2 cups plain flour
1/2 cup icing sugar
150 g unsalted butter

Topping
2 tablespoons dark corn syrup
2 tablespoons cream
1/3 cup soft brown sugar
75 g unsalted butter, melted
2 eggs, lightly beaten
1 teaspoon coffee powder
2 cups pecans

➤ PREHEAT OVEN to moderate 180°C. Brush an 18 x 27 cm shallow rectangular tin with melted butter or oil. Line with baking paper, extending over two sides.

1 Place flour, icing sugar and butter in food processor bowl. Using pulse action, press button for 1 minute or until mixture comes together. Turn out onto a lightly floured surface and knead dough gently for 30 seconds or until smooth. Press into prepared tin and bake for 15 minutes or until it is just golden. Cool completely in tin on a wire rack.

2 For Topping: Combine syrup, cream, sugar, butter, eggs and coffee in a medium mixing bowl and beat with a wooden spoon until smooth. Add pecans and stir to combine.

3 Pour Topping onto pastry base and bake a further 25 minutes, until set. Cool completely in tin. Lift out and cut into squares, using a sharp knife.

COOK'S FILE

Storage time: Slice may be stored for up to five days in an airtight container.
Variation: Use walnuts or macadamia nuts if preferred.
Hints: Corn syrup is a semi-sweet thick syrup, either dark or light, available from most supermarkets. If it is not available, golden syrup can be substituted in this recipe.
Coffee Pecan Slice can be served as a dessert, accompanied by unsweetened whipped cream.

*Continental Fingers (top) and
Coffee Pecan Slice.*

Crazy for CHOCOLATE

MOIST CHOCOLATE BROWNIE

Preparation time: 20 minutes
Total cooking time: 45 minutes
Makes 36 squares

1½ cups plain flour
¼ cup cocoa powder
1 teaspoon baking powder
½ teaspoon bicarbonate of soda
½ cup chopped macadamia nuts
125 g unsalted butter
200 g dark cooking chocolate, chopped
1 cup caster sugar
2 eggs, lightly beaten
⅓ cup sour cream
⅓ cup chopped macadamia nuts, extra

Chocolate Cream Topping
150 g dark cooking chocolate, chopped
½ cup sour cream

➤ PREHEAT OVEN to moderate 180°C. Brush a shallow, 23 cm-square cake tin with melted butter or oil. Line base and sides with paper; grease paper.
1 Sift flour with other dry ingredients into large mixing bowl; add nuts. Make a well in centre.
2 Place butter and chocolate in medium heatproof bowl. Stand over pan of simmering water and stir until chocolate is melted and mixture is smooth. Remove from heat; add sugar, eggs and cream. Beat with a wire whisk until ingredients are well combined and mixture is thick and smooth. Add chocolate mixture to dry ingredients. Using a wooden spoon, stir until well combined; do not overbeat. Spread mixture into prepared tin. Bake 40 minutes or until skewer comes out clean when inserted in centre of slice. Cool in tin.
3 To make Chocolate Cream Topping: Place chocolate in medium heatproof bowl. Stand over pan of simmering water and stir until chocolate is melted. Remove from heat; stand 2 minutes. Add cream and beat with a wire whisk until mixture is thick and glossy. While still warm, spread Chocolate Cream Topping over the slice and sprinkle with nuts; allow to set before cutting into 4 cm squares.

COOK'S FILE

Storage time: Brownies may be stored in an airtight container for up to two days.
Variation: Use pecans or walnuts in place of macadamia nuts.

MOCHA HAZELNUT CRESCENTS

Preparation time: 40 minutes
Total cooking time: 10 minutes
Makes 30

150 g unsalted butter
1/4 cup caster sugar
1 cup plain flour
1/2 cup self-raising flour
2 teaspoons instant coffee
   powder
250 g dark chocolate,
   chopped
1/4 cup ground hazelnuts

➤ PREHEAT OVEN to moderate 180°C. Line a 32 x 28 cm biscuit tray with baking paper.

1 Using electric beaters, beat butter and sugar in a small mixing bowl until mixture is light and creamy. Using a metal spoon, fold in sifted flours and coffee powder and mix to a soft dough.

2 Shape 2 teaspoonsful of mixture into crescents and place on prepared tray. Bake for 10 minutes. Transfer biscuits to a wire rack and allow to cool completely before decorating.

3 Place chocolate in a small heat-proof bowl. Stand over a pan of simmering water and stir until chocolate is melted and mixture smooth. Cool slightly.

4 Working with one at a time, place a crescent into the melted chocolate. Using a spoon, carefully coat the whole crescent in chocolate and lift out on a fork, allowing any excess chocolate to drain away. Place on a wire rack, and sprinkle half the top of the crescent with hazelnuts before the chocolate sets. Repeat with the remaining crescents.

COOK'S FILE

Storage time: Store biscuits in an airtight container for up to three days.

Variation: Use ground almonds. walnuts or other ground nuts of choice in place of the hazelnuts if preferred.

Hint: If the weather is warm, use 250 g compound chocolate or dark chocolate melts in place of the dark chocolate. Compound chocolate will set at room temperature.

CHOCOLATE CHEESE SLICE

Preparation time: 25 minutes
Total cooking time: 50 minutes
Makes 32 bars

1¹/₂ cups plain flour
¹/₄ cup cocoa powder
¹/₂ cup icing sugar
160 g unsalted butter, chopped
1 teaspoon cocoa powder
1 teaspoon icing sugar

Filling
350 g cream cheese

¹/₃ cup sour cream
3 eggs
¹/₃ cup caster sugar
100 g white chocolate, grated

➤ PREHEAT OVEN to moderate 180°C. Brush a 23 cm shallow square cake tin with melted butter or oil. Line base and sides with baking paper, extending it over two sides.

1 Sift flour and other dry ingredients into medium mixing bowl; add butter. Using fingertips, rub butter into flour for 5 minutes or until mixture forms a dough. Press into prepared tin, smooth surface with back of a metal spoon. Bake 15 minutes; allow to cool completely.

2 To make Filling: Place all ingredients in food processor bowl. Using the pulse action, press button for 20 seconds or until mixture is smooth.

3 Pour filling over base. Bake for 35 minutes, until filling is set. Allow to cool completely in tin, then cut into bars. Sift combined cocoa powder and icing sugar onto bars.

COOK'S FILE

Storage time: Store up to three days in an airtight container in the refrigerator.

CHOCOLATE CHESTNUT CREAMS

Preparation time: 25 minutes
Total cooking time: 12 minutes
Makes 35

1 cup plain flour
1 teaspoon cocoa powder
1/4 teaspoon ground cinnamon
50 g unsalted butter
1/3 cup caster sugar
1 egg
200 g choc dots
1 tablespoon vegetable oil
1/3 cup white chocolate
    melts, melted

Chestnut Cream Filling
125 g cream cheese
1/4 cup sweetened chestnut
    spread

➤ PREHEAT OVEN to moderate 180°C. Line two 32 x 28 cm biscuit trays with baking paper.

1 Place flour, cocoa and cinnamon in food processor bowl; add butter and sugar. Using the pulse action, press button for 30 seconds or until mixture is fine and crumbly. Add egg and process 15 seconds or until a soft dough forms.

2 Turn dough onto a lightly floured surface, knead 1 minute until smooth. Roll dough to 4 mm thickness. Cut into 4 cm rounds, using a fluted biscuit cutter. Place on prepared trays. Bake 12 minutes or until lightly golden. Cool biscuits on trays. Place choc dots into a small heatproof bowl. Stand over a pan of simmering water and stir until chocolate is melted; remove from heat. Add oil and beat until mixture is smooth. Cool slightly.

3 To make Chestnut Cream Filling: Using electric beaters, beat cream cheese in small bowl until

light and creamy. Add spread and beat a further 1 minute or until well combined. Spoon filling into a piping bag fitted with a fluted 5 mm-wide piping nozzle and pipe a swirl over each biscuit. Dip each biscuit into melted chocolate, coating the filling and top of biscuit only; place on wire rack to set. Pipe fine lines over each biscuit with white chocolate melts.

COOK'S FILE

Storage time: Store biscuits in an airtight container for up to two days.
Hints: Sweetened chestnut spread is available in cans from some supermarkets, delicatessens and specialty food stores.

A small quantity of vegetable oil enhances the glossy appearance of chocolate used for decorating cakes and biscuits.

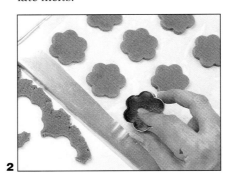

CHOCOLATE DESSERT SLICE

Preparation time: 30 minutes
Total cooking time: 20 minutes +
  2 hours refrigeration
Makes 16

200 g dark chocolate cream
  biscuits
50 g unsalted butter, melted
1 cup milk
3 egg yolks
1/3 cup caster sugar
2 tablespoons cornflour
1/4 cup cocoa powder
1 tablespoon marsala
1 cup (250 g) mascarpone
  cheese
1 tablespoon boiling water
2 1/2 teaspoons gelatine
50 g white chocolate

➤ PREHEAT OVEN to moderate 180°C. Brush a 20 cm shallow square cake tin with melted butter or oil. Line base and sides with baking paper, extending over two sides.

1 Place biscuits in food processor bowl. Using the pulse action, press button for 30 seconds or until biscuits are finely crushed. Add butter and process further 15–20 seconds or until combined. Press mixture firmly into base of prepared tin. Bake 10 minutes; remove from oven and cool completely.

2 Heat milk in a small pan until almost boiling. Remove from heat. Whisk egg yolks, sugar, cornflour, cocoa and 2 tablespoons of the milk in a small mixing bowl until creamy. Add remaining milk gradually, beating constantly. Strain mixture into pan. Stir over a low heat 3 minutes until mixture thickens slightly and coats the back of a wooden spoon. Remove custard from heat; stir in marsala. Transfer mixture to a medium mixing bowl. Cover surface with plastic wrap and allow to cool to lukewarm. Fold mascarpone into custard until completely combined.

3 Combine gelatine with boiling water in a small bowl. Stand bowl in hot water; stir until dissolved. Add gelatine to custard and stir until completly combined. Pour custard onto biscuit base, cover with plastic wrap and refrigerate for 2 hours.

4 When custard has set, carefully lift slice from tin. Cut edges neatly away from paper. Cut slice into squares with a sharp knife. Using a vegetable peeler, shave off chocolate from side of block. Decorate each slice with white chocolate shavings.

COOK'S FILE

Storage time: Slice will keep up to two days stored in an airtight container in the refrigerator. Decorate just before serving.

Variation: Substitute another liqueur or spirit, such as a coffee liqueur or rum, for the marsala if desired.

CHOCOLATE JAMAICAN ROUNDS

Preparation time: 15 minutes
Total cooking time: 25 minutes
Makes 30

100 g unsalted butter
1/3 cup caster sugar
1 teaspoon coconut essence
2 tablespoons coconut cream
60 g milk chocolate, melted
2 teaspoons grated lime rind
1/2 cup desiccated coconut
1 3/4 cups plain flour
2 tablespoons desiccated coconut, extra

Icing
60 g grated dark cooking chocolate, chopped
30 g unsalted butter
2 teaspoons coconut cream
1/4 teaspoon coconut essence

➤ PREHEAT OVEN to moderate 180°C. Line a 32 x 28 cm biscuit tray with baking paper.

1 Using electric beaters, beat butter and sugar in small mixing bowl until light and creamy. Add essence, cream, chocolate and rind; beat until well combined.

2 Add coconut and flour and press together to form a soft dough. Turn onto a lightly floured surface; knead 1 minute or until smooth.

3 Roll three teaspoons of mixture at a time into balls. Place on prepared tray. Flatten slightly, using the base of a glass. Bake 20 minutes or until lightly browned. Cool biscuits on tray.

4 To make Icing: Place chocolate and butter in small heatproof bowl. Stand over pan of simmering water and stir until chocolate is melted and mixture smooth. Remove from heat. Add cream and essence and stir to combine. When biscuits cool, dip tops in icing. Sprinkle with extra coconut; allow to set.

COOK'S FILE

Storage time: Biscuits may be stored in an airtight container for up to two days.
Variation: Decorate with melted white or milk chocolate in place of the dark chocolate.

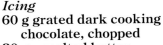

CHOCOLATE CHERRY OATIES

Preparation time: 12 minutes
Total cooking time: 15 minutes
Makes 30

1/4 cup plain flour
1/4 cup self-raising flour
1 1/2 cup rolled oats
1/2 cup caster sugar
1/2 cup chopped pecan nuts
1/2 cup glacé cherries, quartered
1/4 cup choc dots

1/3 cup chopped white chocolate
125 g unsalted butter, melted
2 eggs, lightly beaten
80 g white chocolate melts, melted

➤ PREHEAT OVEN to moderate 180°C. Line 32 x 28 cm biscuit tray with baking paper.

1 Sift flours into large mixing bowl; add oats, sugar, nuts, cherries and chocolate, stir. Make a well in the centre; add butter and eggs.

2 Using a flat-bladed knife, stir until all ingredients are well combined.

3 Drop one level tablespoon of mixture at a time onto prepared tray, allowing room for spreading. Bake 12–15 minutes or until lightly browned. Transfer to wire rack to cool. Pipe a spiral of white chocolate on top of each biscuit.

COOK'S FILE

Storage time: Store in an airtight container for up to two days.
Variation: Use any kind of nut to replace the pecans.
Hint: Choc dots are available from the supermarket.

Chocolate Jamaican Rounds (top) and Chocolate Cherry Oaties.

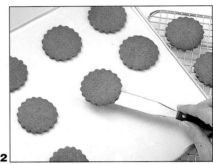

CHOCOLATE CARAMEL ROUNDS

Preparation time: 30 minutes
Total cooking time: 25 minutes
Makes 30

1¹/2 cups plain flour
1 tablespoon cocoa powder
180 g unsalted butter,
    chopped
1/2 cup soft brown sugar
1 egg yolk
2 tablespoons grated milk
    chocolate
200 g (1 cup) choc bits,
30 choc bits, extra

Caramel Filling
200 g jersey caramels,
    chopped
1 tablespoon unsalted butter
1 tablespoon cream

➤ PREHEAT OVEN to moderate
180°C. Line two 32 x 28 cm biscuit
trays with baking paper.

1 Sift flour and cocoa powder into
large mixing bowl; add butter and
sugar. Using your fingertips, rub butter into the flour for 2 minutes or
until mixture is fine and crumbly.
Add egg yolk and grated chocolate
and press together to form a soft
dough. Turn dough onto a lightly
floured surface and knead for
1 minute.

2 Roll pastry to 6 mm thickness. Cut
into 5 cm rounds, using a fluted biscuit cutter; place on prepared tray.
Bake 15 minutes. Transfer biscuits to
wire rack to cool.

3 To make Caramel Filling:
Combine caramels, butter and cream
in a small pan. Stir over low heat
for 3 minutes or until caramels have
melted; remove from heat and beat
until smooth. Cool.

4 To melt choc bits for top of the
biscuits, place in a small heatproof
bowl. Stand bowl over a pan of simmering water and stir until chocolate
is melted and smooth. To assemble
biscuits, spread a little melted chocolate over each. Place half a teaspoon

of Caramel Filling in the centre of
each biscuit. Push one of the extra
choc bits into the centre of each biscuit.

COOK'S FILE

Storage time: Biscuits may be
stored in an airtight container for up
to two days.
Variation: Sandwich a small quantity of melted chocolate and Caramel
Filling between two biscuits instead
of putting them on top. Repeat with
remaining biscuits.

CHOCOLATE APRICOT PRETZELS

Preparation time: 25 minutes
Total cooking time: 20 minutes
Makes 40

1/2 cup (80 g) finely chopped dried apricots
1/3 cup orange juice
20 g unsalted butter
3/4 cup self-raising flour
1/2 cup plain flour
60 g unsalted butter, chopped
1/4 cup caster sugar
2 egg yolks

1/2 cup (70 g) grated milk chocolate
150 g white chocolate melts
10 g white vegetable shortening

➤ PREHEAT OVEN to moderate 180°C. Line a 32 x 28 cm biscuit tray with baking paper.

1 Combine apricots, juice and butter in small pan. Stir over low heat 5 minutes; remove from heat, cool.

2 Sift flours into large mixing bowl; add butter and sugar. Using finger-tips, rub butter into flour for 2 minutes or until mixture is fine and crumbly. Add yolks, chocolate and cooled apricot mixture. Press mix-

ture together to form a soft dough.

3 Turn onto lightly floured surface, knead 2 minutes until smooth. Roll two level teaspoons of mixture at a time into balls. Roll dough into 15 cm x 5 mm lengths. Shape and loop into pretzels. Bake 15 minutes or until lightly browned. Transfer to wire rack to cool. Combine chocolate melts and shortening; stir over low heat until melted. Dip half of each pretzel diagonally in the melted chocolate mixture .

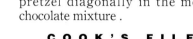
COOK'S FILE

Storage time: Store pretzels in an airtight container for up to two days.

1

2

3

CHOC-MINT SWIRLS

Preparation time: 30 minutes
Total cooking time: 15 minutes
Makes 22

65 g unsalted butter
1/4 cup caster sugar
1/2 cup plain flour
1/3 cup self-raising flour
2 tablespoons cocoa
    powder
1–2 tablespoons milk
22 choc bits

Filling
100 g unsalted butter, extra

1 1/3 cups icing sugar
few drops peppermint essence

➤ PREHEAT OVEN to 180°C. Line two 32 x 28 cm biscuit trays with baking paper.

1 Using electric beaters, beat butter and sugar in a small mixing bowl until light and creamy. Add sifted flours, cocoa and milk. Stir with a flat-bladed knife until mixture forms a soft dough. Turn out onto a piece of baking paper; knead for 1 minute or until smooth.

2 Roll dough out to 5 mm thickness. Cut into rounds, using a 4 cm plain biscuit cutter. Place on prepared tray and bake for 15 minutes. Transfer to a wire rack to cool completely before decorating.

3 To make Filling: Using electric beaters, beat butter until soft. Add icing sugar and beat until smooth, creamy and light. Add essence; beat until combined. Using a piping bag fitted with a large fluted nozzle, pipe a flower of peppermint cream onto each biscuit. Place a choc bit in the centre of each flower.

COOK'S FILE

Storage time: Store up to two days in an airtight container.
Variation: Dust biscuits with one teaspoon each of icing sugar and cocoa powder, sifted together.

1

2

3

CINNAMON PECAN BISCUITS

Preparation time: 20 minutes
Total cooking time: 15 minutes
Makes 40

100 g dark chocolate
125 g unsalted butter
1/2 cup caster sugar
1 egg, lightly beaten
3/4 cup finely chopped pecans
1/3 cup self-raising flour
2/3 cup plain flour
2 teaspoons ground cinnamon
1/2 cup (50 g) whole pecans, for
 decoration
1 tablespoon icing sugar, for
 dusting

➤ PREHEAT OVEN to moderate
180°C. Line two 32 x 28 cm biscuit
trays with baking paper.
1 Chop chocolate and place in a
small heatproof bowl. Stand over a
pan of simmering water. Stir until
chocolate is melted and smooth.
Allow to cool but not to reset.
2 Using electric beaters, beat butter
and sugar in a small mixing bowl
until light and creamy. Add egg
gradually, beating thoroughly. Add
cooled melted chocolate and beat
until combined.
3 Transfer mixture to large mixing
bowl; add pecans. Using a metal
spoon, fold in sifted flours and cinnamon. Stir until ingredients are combined; do not overbeat. Lightly roll
2 teaspoonsful of mixture into oval
shapes, place on prepared tray and
press a pecan onto each. Bake for
10 minutes.
4 Transfer to wire rack to cool.
Place icing sugar in a sieve, and
lightly dust each biscuit.

COOK'S FILE

Storage time: Biscuits may be
stored for up to two days in an airtight container.
Hint: If liked, bake biscuits without
the pecan on top. When baked and
cooled, dip top of each biscuit in
melted chocolate and press a pecan
on top.
Variations: Use ground mixed spice
or allspice in place of the cinnamon if
preferred.
Walnuts may be substituted for
pecans in this recipe.

1

2

3

4

SACHER SQUARES

Preparation time: 1 hour
Total cooking time: 40 minutes
Makes 24

Base
1 cup plain flour
60 g unsalted butter, chopped
1/4 cup sugar
2 egg yolks, lightly beaten
2 teaspoons iced water

Cake
1 cup plain flour
1/3 cup cocoa powder
1 cup caster sugar
100 g unsalted butter
2 tablespoons apricot jam
4 eggs, separated
1 cup apricot jam, extra

Topping
250 g dark chocolate
3/4 cup cream

➤ PREHEAT OVEN to moderate 180°C. Cut an 18 x 27 cm rectangle of baking paper.

1 To make Base: Sift flour into a large mixing bowl; add butter. Using fingertips, rub butter into flour for 3 minutes or until fine and crumbly. Using a wooden spoon, stir in sugar. Add egg yolks and almost all the water and mix to a firm dough, adding more liquid if necessary. Turn onto a lightly floured surface and knead 30 seconds or until smooth. Roll out pastry and cut to fit baking paper. Place on large flat biscuit tray and bake 10 minutes or until just golden. Cool completely.

2 To make Cake: Preheat oven to moderate 180°C. Brush an 18 x 28 cm shallow rectangular tin with melted butter or oil and line base and sides with baking paper, extending over two sides. Sift flour and cocoa into a large mixing bowl. Make a well in the centre. Combine sugar, butter and jam in a small pan. Stir over a low heat until butter has melted and sugar has dissolved; remove from heat. Add butter mixture to dry ingredients. Stir until just combined; add egg yolks and mix well.

3 Place egg whites in a small, clean, dry mixing bowl. Using electric beaters, beat until soft peaks form. Using a metal spoon, fold egg whites into cake mixture. Pour into prepared tin, bake for 30 minutes or until a skewer comes out clean when inserted into centre of cake. Leave cake in tin 15 minutes before turning out onto a wire rack to cool.

4 Warm jam in microwave or over a pan of simmering water; push through a fine sieve. Brush pastry base with quarter cup of the jam. Place cake on base. Trim each side evenly, cutting 'crust' from cake and base. Using a sharp knife, cut into 24 squares.

5 Brush top and sides of each square with apricot jam. Place squares on a large wire rack, over a piece of baking paper, leaving at least 4 cm between each.

6 To make Topping: Break chocolate into small pieces and place in a small bowl. Place cream in a small pan and bring to the boil. Remove from heat. Pour over chocolate and stir until chocolate is melted and mixture smooth. Cool slightly. Working one at a time, pour topping over each square and use a flat-bladed knife to cover completely. Scrape excess topping from paper, with any left over, and spoon into a small paper piping bag. Seal open end, snip off tip and pipe an 'S' onto each square.

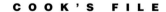
COOK'S FILE

Storage time: Store up to five days in an airtight container.

4

5

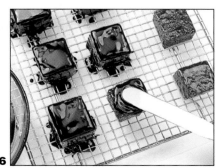

6

CHOCOLATE LEMON SWIRLS

Preparation time: 12 minutes
Total cooking time: 12 minutes
Makes 60

125 g unsalted butter
2/3 cup icing sugar
1 egg, lightly beaten
2 teaspoons grated lemon rind
1¼ cups plain flour
¼ cup cocoa powder

2 tablespoons finely chopped mixed peel

➤ PREHEAT OVEN to moderate 180°C. Line a 32 x 28 cm biscuit tray with baking paper.

1 Using electric beaters, beat butter and sugar until light and creamy. Add egg and rind, beat until well combined.

2 Add flour and cocoa. Using a metal spoon, stir until ingredients are just combined and mixture is almost smooth.

3 Spoon mixture into a piping bag fitted with a fluted 1 cm-wide piping nozzle; pipe swirls about 3 cm in diameter onto prepared tray. Top each swirl with mixed peel. Bake for 12 minutes; cool biscuits on trays.

COOK'S FILE

Storage time: Biscuits may be stored in an airtight container for up to two days.

Variation: Use orange rind in place of the lemon rind, if preferred.

CHOC-VANILLA CREAMS

Preparation time: 45 minutes
Total cooking time: 10 minutes
Makes 15

125 g unsalted butter
1/3 cup icing sugar
2/3 cup plain flour
1/2 cup self-raising flour
2 tablespoons cocoa
    powder
2/3 cup chocolate sprinkles
2 teaspoons icing sugar for
    dusting

Vanilla Cream
75 g unsalted butter

2/3 cup icing sugar
1 teaspoon vanilla essence

➤ PREHEAT OVEN to moderate 180°C. Line a 32 x 28 cm biscuit tray with baking paper.

1 Using electric beaters, beat butter and sugar in a small mixing bowl until light and creamy. Using a metal spoon, fold in sifted flours and cocoa and mix to a soft dough. Roll 2 teaspoonsful of dough into balls. Using the base of a glass, press into 4 cm rounds. Place on prepared tray. Bake for 10 minutes. Transfer biscuits to a wire rack to cool completely before decorating.

2 To make Vanilla Cream: Using electric beaters, beat butter and sugar until light and creamy. Add essence; beat until combined.

3 To assemble biscuits, spread one biscuit with vanilla cream and place another on top to sandwich together. Using a flat-bladed knife, spread vanilla cream around the join.

4 Place chocolate sprinkles on a plate and roll each biscuit on the side to coat join. Dust with icing sugar.

COOK'S FILE

Storage time: Will keep up to two days in an airtight container.

TRIPLE CHOCOLATE PEANUT BUTTER COOKIES

Preparation time: 20 minutes
Total cooking time: 30 minutes
Makes about 34

125 g unsalted butter
3/4 cup soft brown sugar
1 egg, lightly beaten
3/4 cup peanut butter
1 cup plain flour
1/2 teaspoon bicarbonate
   of soda
1/4 cup cocoa powder
175 g white chocolate melts
175 g dark chocolate melts

➤ PREHEAT OVEN to moderate 180°C. Line two 32 x 28 cm biscuit trays with baking paper.
1 Using electric beaters, beat butter and sugar in a medium mixing bowl until light and creamy. Add egg gradually, beating thoroughly after each addition. Add peanut butter and beat until combined.
2 Using a metal spoon, add sifted flour, soda and cocoa; mix to a soft dough. Roll level tablespoons of mixture into balls. Place on prepared trays and flatten with a fork in a criss-cross pattern. Bake for 20 minutes. Cool on trays for 5 minutes before transferring to wire racks. Allow biscuits to cool completely before decorating.

3 Place white chocolate melts in a small heatproof bowl. Stand over simmering water and stir until chocolate is melted and smooth. Dip one-third of each cookie in white chocolate. Place on wire rack to set. Melt the dark chocolate melts in the same way, and dip the opposite one-third of each cookie, leaving a plain band in the centre.

COOK'S FILE

Storage time: Cookies may be stored for up to three days in an airtight container.
Hints: Sprinkle biscuits with crushed nuts if desired.
Crunchy or smooth peanut butter may be used, as preferred.

1

2

3

JAFFA RINGS

Preparation time: 30 minutes
Total cooking time: 20 minutes
Makes about 45

180 g unsalted butter
¹/2 cup caster sugar
1 egg, lightly beaten
1¹/2 teaspoons finely grated
orange rind
50 g milk chocolate, grated
1 cup self-raising flour
2 cups plain flour
100 g milk chocolate melts

➤ PREHEAT OVEN to moderate 180°C. Line two 32 x 28 cm biscuit trays with baking paper.

1 Using electric beaters, beat butter, sugar and egg until light and creamy. Add rind and grated chocolate; beat until combined.

2 Transfer the mixture to a large mixing bowl. Using a flat-bladed knife, fold in sifted flours and mix together to form a soft dough. Turn onto a lightly floured surface and knead for 30 seconds or until the dough is smooth.

3 Roll 3 teaspoonsful of mixture into small oblongs. Continue rolling into lengths of 20 cm. Carefully fold in half and twist. Form twisted rope into a ring. Place on prepared trays. Bake for 12 minutes and transfer to a wire rack to cool.

4 Place milk chocolate melts in a small heatproof bowl. Stand over pan of simmering water and stir until the chocolate is melted and smooth. Cool slightly. Dip bases of the biscuits into melted chocolate. Stand on wire rack to set.

COOK'S FILE

Storage time: Biscuits may be kept up to four days in an airtight container.
Hint: To decorate these biscuits quickly, melted chocolate can be simply drizzled off the end of the prongs of a fork.

CHOC-HAZELNUT SCROLLS

Preparation time: 25 minutes
Total cooking time: 15 minutes +
  30 minutes refrigeration
Makes 35

2 cups plain flour
1/2 cup ground hazelnuts
100 g unsalted butter, chopped
1/2 cup caster sugar
1 egg, lightly beaten
2 tablespoons iced water
1/4 cup chocolate hazelnut
  spread

▶ LINE TWO 32 x 28 cm biscuit trays with baking paper.

1 Place dry ingredients in food processor bowl; add butter and sugar. Using the pulse action, press button for 30 seconds or until mixture is fine and crumbly. Add combined egg and water; process a further 20 seconds until mixture forms a dough. Turn out onto a lightly floured surface and knead 30 seconds or until smooth.

2 Roll pastry out on a large sheet of baking paper, to a rectangle of 25 x 35 cm. Trim any uneven edges. Spread dough evenly with hazelnut spread. Using paper to lift dough, roll up from the long side in Swiss roll style. Wrap tightly in paper and refrigerate for 30 minutes.

3 Heat oven to moderate 180°C. Cut dough into 1 cm slices, wiping blade of knife between cuts. Place on prepared trays; bake 15 minutes. Transfer to wire rack to cool.

COOK'S FILE

Storage time: Store in an airtight container for up to three days.
Variation: Use ground macadamia nuts in place of the hazelnuts.
Hint: Chocolate hazelnut spread can be found in the jam and spread section of most supermarkets.

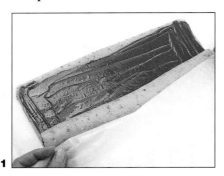

COCOA SESAME BISCUITS

Preparation time: 15 minutes
Total cooking time: 12 minutes
Makes about 33

3/4 cup plain flour
1/4 cup cocoa powder
3/4 cup rolled oats
1 cup sesame seeds
3/4 cup caster sugar
100 g unsalted butter
2 tablespoons golden syrup
1 tablespoon boiling water
1 teaspoon bicarbonate of soda
185 g milk chocolate melts,
  melted

▶ PREHEAT OVEN to moderately slow 160°C. Line two 32 x 28 cm biscuit trays with baking paper.

1 Sift flour with cocoa into large mixing bowl. Add oats, seeds and sugar; make a well in the centre.

2 Combine butter and golden syrup in a small pan. Stir over a low heat until butter is melted and mixture smooth; remove from heat. Pour boiling water into a small bowl; add soda. Stir until soda has dissolved. Add to golden syrup mixture. Using a metal spoon, fold mixture into the dry ingredients. Stir until well combined.

3 Drop three level tablespoons of mixture onto prepared trays, allowing room for spreading. Flatten each one slightly with fingertips. Bake 12 minutes and cool biscuits on trays for 5 minutes before transferring to a wire rack to cool completely. Spread approximately one teaspoon of chocolate into 3 cm round in the centre of each biscuit.

COOK'S FILE

Storage time: Biscuits may be stored in an airtight container for up to one week.
Hints: For extra chocolate flavour, add two tablespoons of dark chocolate chips to mixture, or drizzle the biscuits with melted dark chocolate. Cocoa powder varies in colour; the darker the colour, the richer the flavour will be.

Choc-Hazelnut Scrolls (top) and Cocoa Sesame Biscuits.

BRANDY ALEXANDER SLICE

Preparation time: 20 minutes
Total cooking time: 5 minutes
Makes 12 bars

80 g unsalted butter, chopped
60 g dark cooking chocolate, chopped
250 g packet plain chocolate biscuits, crushed
300 g ricotta cheese
¼ cup cream
⅓ cup icing sugar, sifted
½ cup grated milk chocolate
1 tablespoon brandy
1 tablespoon créme de caçao liqueur
½ teaspoon ground nutmeg
60 g dark chocolate melts

➤ BRUSH A SHALLOW 30 x 20 cm rectangular tin with melted butter or oil. Line base and sides with baking paper.

1 Place butter and chocolate in small heatproof bowl. Stand over pan of simmering water. Stir until chocolate is melted and mixture is smooth. Remove from heat. Using a flat-bladed knife, mix chocolate mixture with the biscuit crumbs in a small bowl.

2 Press biscuit mixture evenly over base of prepared tin; set aside.

3 Using electric beaters, beat cheese, cream and sugar in small mixing bowl on medium speed 3 minutes or until mixture is light and creamy. Add chocolate, brandy and liqueur. Beat on low speed further 1 minute.

4 Spread cheese mixture over prepared base; sprinkle with nutmeg.

Refrigerate several hours or overnight. Cut into 12 bars before serving. Place chocolate melts in small heatproof bowl and stand over simmering water until chocolate is melted. Use to pipe design on top of each bar.

COOK'S FILE

Storage time: Store in an airtight container in the refrigerator for up to two days.
Variation: Use Tia Maria in place of the créme de caçao.

CHOC-BANANA CHIP BISCUITS

Preparation time: 20 minutes
Total cooking time: 20 minutes
Makes about 40

150 g banana chips, crushed
1/4 cup plain flour
1/4 cup self-raising flour
2 tablespoons cocoa powder
1/2 cup caster sugar
40 g unsalted butter, melted
2 eggs, lightly beaten
60 g dark chocolate melts

➤ PREHEAT OVEN to moderate 180°C. Line two 32 x 28 cm biscuit trays with baking paper.

1 Reserve 40 small banana chips (about 50 g) for decoration and place the rest in food processor bowl. Using pulse action, press button for 20 seconds or until chips are like coarse breadcrumbs.

2 Sift flours with cocoa powder and caster sugar into mixing bowl; add banana chips. Make well in centre. Stir in melted butter and eggs. Using a metal spoon, mix until well combined. Do not overbeat.

3 Drop 2 teaspoonsful of mixture onto prepared trays, top each with a banana chip. Bake for 15 minutes; cool on trays for 10 minutes before transferring to a wire rack to cool completely. Place chocolate melts in small heatproof bowl over simmering water until melted. Use to pipe design on top of each biscuits.

COOK'S FILE

Storage time: Biscuits may be stored for up to two days in an airtight container.

Hint: Banana chips are available from supermarkets and health food stores.

1

2

3

Irresistible FRUIT & NUT TREATS

CHOCOLATE CARROT SLICE

Preparation time: 15 minutes
Total cooking time: 30 minutes
Makes 32

1 cup self-raising flour
1 teaspoon ground cinnamon
3/4 cup caster sugar
1/2 cup finely grated carrot
1 cup mixed dried fruit
1/2 cup choc bits
1/3 cup desiccated coconut
2 eggs, lightly beaten
90 g unsalted butter, melted
1/3 cup chopped walnuts

Cream Cheese Frosting
125 g cream cheese
30 g unsalted butter
1 1/2 cups icing sugar, sifted
1 teaspoon hot water

➤ PREHEAT OVEN to moderate 180°C. Brush a shallow 23 cm square cake tin with melted butter or oil and line the base and sides with baking paper.
1 Sift flour and cinnamon into a large mixing bowl. Add caster sugar, grated carrot, mixed fruit, choc bits and coconut and stir until just combined. Add beaten eggs and butter. Stir until the mixture is just combined.
2 Spread mixture evenly into prepared tin and smooth surface. Bake for 30 minutes or until golden. Cool in tin; turn out.
3 To make Cream Cheese Frosting: Using electric beaters, beat cream cheese and butter in small mixing bowl until smooth. Add icing sugar and beat for 2 minutes or until mixture is light and fluffy. Add water; beat until combined. Spread slice with frosting using a flat-bladed knife and sprinkle with walnuts. Cut into 16 squares, then cut each square into triangles.

COOK'S FILE

Storage time: Slice may be stored for up to two days in an airtight container or up to two months in the freezer, without icing.
Hint: Sprinkle the Cream Cheese Frosting with grated chocolate if desired. This slice is also delicious without icing.

PEANUT BUTTER COOKIES

Preparation time: 15 minutes
Total cooking time: 10 minutes
Makes about 30

1 cup plain flour
1/2 cup self-raising flour
1 cup rolled oats
125 g unsalted butter
1/2 cup caster sugar
1/3 cup honey
2 tablespoons peanut
   butter

1 cup roasted unsalted peanuts,
   finely chopped

Topping:
3/4 cup icing sugar
25 g butter, softened
1 tablespoon warm water

➤ PREHEAT OVEN to moderate 180°C. Brush two baking trays with melted butter or oil.
1 Sift flours into a large mixing bowl; stir in oats.
2 Combine butter, sugar, honey and peanut butter in pan and stir over medium heat until melted. Add to flour mixture. Using a metal spoon, stir to just combine ingredients. Roll heaped teaspoons of mixture into balls. Arrange on prepared trays, with room for spreading, and press lightly to flatten. Bake 10 minutes or until golden. Cool cookies on trays.
3 To make Topping: Combine icing sugar, butter and water in small bowl. Stir until smooth. Dip tops of cookies into topping, then into nuts.

COOK'S FILE

Storage time: Store up to four days in an airtight container or up to three months in the freezer, without icing.

CRUNCHY APPLE SLICE

Preparation time: 30 minutes
Total cooking time: 1 hour
Makes 18

2¹/2 cups plain flour
125 g unsalted butter
¹/3 cup water
¹/2 cup marmalade
¹/4 cup ground hazelnuts
410 g can pie apple
¹/4 teaspoon ground mixed
 spice
2 tablespoons sugar

➤ PREHEAT OVEN to moderate 180°C. Brush a shallow 23 cm square cake tin with melted butter or oil.
1 Place flour and butter in food processor bowl. Using pulse action, press the button for 20 seconds or until the mixture is fine and crumbly. Add water to bowl. Process 5 seconds or until combined. Turn out onto a lightly floured surface; knead 1 minute or until smooth.
2 Press out two-thirds of the mixture large enough to cover base of prepared tin. Place remaining one-third in freezer for about 20 minutes. Spread pastry base in tin with mar-malade. Sprinkle with hazelnuts.
3 Spoon apple evenly over hazelnuts and sprinkle with spice.
4 Coarsely grate reserved pastry and sprinkle evenly over apple. Sprinkle with sugar. Bake for 1 hour or until golden. Cool slice in tin. Cut into fingers when cold.

COOK'S FILE

Storage time: Store up to three days in an airtight container.
Hint: Any ground nuts can be used; try walnuts or pecans.

SPICY WHOLEMEAL TWISTS

Preparation time: 20 minutes
Total cooking time: 15 minutes
Makes about 40

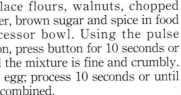

1 cup self-raising flour
1/2 cup wholemeal self-raising flour
1/4 cup ground walnuts
125 g unsalted butter, chopped
1/3 cup soft brown sugar
3 teaspoons mixed spice
1 egg, lightly beaten
1 tablespoon sugar

➤ PREHEAT OVEN to moderate 180°C. Brush two 32 x 28 cm biscuit trays with melted butter or oil.

1 Place flours, walnuts, chopped butter, brown sugar and spice in food processor bowl. Using the pulse action, press button for 10 seconds or until the mixture is fine and crumbly. Add egg; process 10 seconds or until just combined.

2 Transfer mixture to a medium bowl; press ingredients together to form a soft dough. Cover with plastic wrap; refrigerate for 30 minutes or until mixture is firm.

3 Roll 2 teaspoons of mixture into 14 cm lengths. Fold lengths in half.

Twist and press ends together. Place onto prepared trays. Sprinkle with sugar. Bake for 15 minutes or until golden. Transfer biscuits to wire rack to cool.

COOK'S FILE

Storage time: Biscuits may be stored up to four days in an airtight container or up to two months in the freezer.
Variation: Dust biscuits with icing sugar when cold.
Hint: Ground walnuts are found in supermarkets and delicatessens, or they may be freshly ground in the food processor or blender.

CITRUS COOKIES

Preparation time: 10 minutes
Total cooking time: 15 minutes
Makes about 30

125 g unsalted butter
3/4 cup icing sugar, sifted
1 1/2 cups plain flour
2 teaspoons finely grated lime rind
2 teaspoons finely grated lemon rind
1/3 cup sour cream
1 tablespoon lemon juice

Orange Icing
1 cup pure icing sugar

2 teaspoons finely grated orange rind
2 tablespoons orange juice

➤ PREHEAT OVEN to moderate 180°C. Brush two 32 x 28 cm biscuit trays with melted butter or oil.

1 Place butter, icing sugar, flour, grated lime and lemon rinds in bowl of food processor. Using the pulse action, press button for 10 seconds or until the mixture is fine and crumbly. Add sour cream and lemon juice and process for 10 seconds or until mixture is well combined.

2 Drop level tablespoons of mixture onto prepared trays, allowing room for spreading. Bake for 15 minutes or

until lightly golden. Transfer cookies to wire rack to cool.

3 To make Orange Icing: Combine icing sugar, orange rind and juice in a small bowl. Stand bowl over pan of simmering water, stirring until icing is smooth and glossy; remove from heat. Spread icing over cookies with a flat-bladed knife; stand until set.

COOK'S FILE

Storage time: Store cookies up to three days in an airtight container or up to two months in the freezer, without icing.
Hint: Overbeating the icing will make it dull, flat and grainy. Work quickly with icing. Do not reheat.

Spicy Wholemeal Twists (top) and Citrus Cookies.

GINGER AND PISTACHIO SQUARES

Preparation time: 20 minutes
Total cooking time: 35 minutes
Makes 28

125 g unsalted butter
1 cup soft brown sugar
2 eggs, lightly beaten
1¼ cups self-raising flour
6 teaspoons ground ginger

White Chocolate Icing
150 g white chocolate, chopped
¼ cup cream
2 tablespoons chopped glacé
   ginger
2 tablespoons chopped
   pistachio nuts

➤ PREHEAT OVEN to moderate
180°C.
1 Brush a shallow 27 x 18 cm rectangular cake tin with melted butter or oil. Cover base with baking paper, extending over two sides; grease paper.
2 Using electric beaters, beat butter and sugar in a small mixing bowl until light and creamy. Add eggs gradually, beating thoroughly after each addition. Transfer mixture to a large mixing bowl. Using a metal spoon, fold in the sifted flour and ginger and stir until just combined.
3 Spread mixture into the prepared tin. Bake for 30 minutes or until golden and firm in the centre. Allow slice to cool in the tin before turning out.
4 **To make White Chocolate Icing:** Combine chocolate and cream in small pan. Stir over low heat until chocolate has melted and mixture is smooth. Cool. Using a flat-bladed knife, spread icing evenly over slice. Sprinkle with ginger and pistachio nuts; allow icing to set, then cut into squares.

COOK'S FILE

Storage time: Slice may be stored for up to three days in an airtight container or up to two months in the freezer without icing.
Variation: Any chopped nuts, such as walnuts, pecans or toasted almonds are suitable for this recipe. If preferred, ice with lemon icing.

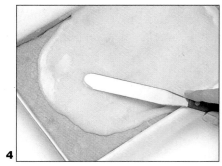

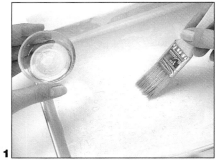

COCONUT PINEAPPLE SQUARES

Preparation time: 20 minutes
Total cooking time: 20 minutes
Makes 24

250 g oatmeal biscuits, crushed
1 cup shredded coconut
1 cup (250 g) chopped glacé
    pineapple
1 cup flaked almonds
200 ml condensed milk
100 g unsalted butter, melted

Coconut Icing
60 g butter, softened

few drops coconut essence
3/4 cup icing sugar, sifted
1 tablespoon milk
3/4 cup toasted flaked
    coconut

➤ PREHEAT OVEN to moderate 180°C. Brush a shallow 27 x 18 cm rectangular cake tin with melted butter or oil; line base with paper; grease the paper.

1 Combine biscuits, coconut, pineapple and almonds in large mixing bowl. Make well in the centre. Add condensed milk and butter; stir until combined.

2 Press mixture into the prepared tin. Bake for 20 minutes or until top is lightly golden; cool.

3 **To make Coconut Icing:** With electric beaters, beat butter and essence in a small mixing bowl until light and creamy. Add icing sugar and milk; beat until the mixture is smooth and fluffy. Spread slice evenly with icing; sprinkle with toasted coconut. Cut into squares.

COOK'S FILE

Storage time: Slice may be stored for up to three days in an airtight container or up to two months in the freezer, without icing.
Hint: To toast coconut: Spread onto an oven tray; cook in moderate oven for five minutes or until golden.

APPLE AND CINNAMON OATCAKES

Preparation time: 15 minutes
Total cooking time: 20 minutes
Makes about 20

1 cup chopped dried apple
½ cup boiling water
125 g unsalted butter
½ cup soft brown sugar
1 egg, lightly beaten
¾ cup rolled oats
¼ cup desiccated coconut
1 cup self-raising flour
1 tablespoon cinnamon sugar

➤ PREHEAT OVEN to moderate 180°C. Brush two 32 x 28 cm biscuit trays with melted butter or oil. Combine apples and water in small bowl; stand 5 minutes or until all water is absorbed.

1 Using electric beaters, beat butter and sugar in small mixing bowl until light and creamy. Add egg and beat thoroughly.

2 Transfer mixture to large mixing bowl; add oats, coconut, apple and sifted flour. Using a metal spoon, stir until just combined.

3 Drop heaped tablespoonfuls of mixture onto prepared trays, allowing sufficient room for spreading.

Sprinkle with cinnamon sugar. Bake for 20 minutes or until biscuits are lightly golden. Transfer to wire racks to cool.

COOK'S FILE

Storage time: Biscuits may be stored for two days in an airtight container or up to two months in the freezer.

Hint: Cinnamon sugar may be obtained from supermarkets, or make your own by combining equal quantities of caster sugar and ground cinnamon.

Variation: Use chopped dried apricots instead of apples.

CHERRY COCONUT SQUARES

Preparation time: 20 minutes
Total cooking time: 25 minutes
Makes 30

1 cup self-raising flour
1 cup desiccated coconut
1/2 cup caster sugar
125 g unsalted butter, melted
50 g dark chocolate

Cherry Topping
1 cup finely chopped glacé
  cherries

1/4 cup soft brown sugar
1/2 cup desiccated coconut,
  extra
1/2 cup chopped pecan nuts
2 eggs, lightly beaten

➤ PREHEAT OVEN to moderate 180°C. Brush a 30 x 25 x 2 cm shallow Swiss roll tin with melted butter or oil.

1 Combine sifted flour, coconut and sugar in a medium mixing bowl. Add butter and stir until combined. Press mixture into prepared tin.

2 To make Cherry Topping: Combine cherries, brown sugar, extra coconut and pecans in a medium mixing bowl. Add eggs; stir until combined. Spread evenly over base in the tin.

3 Bake for 20 minutes or until top is lightly golden. Cool in tin. Place chocolate in small heatproof bowl over simmering water and stir until chocolate is melted and smooth. Drizzle chocolate in crisscross pattern over top. Cut into 5 x 5 cm squares.

COOK'S FILE

Storage time: Store for up to three days in an airtight container or up to two months in the freezer.

PRUNE AND CREAM CHEESE SCROLLS

Preparation time: 30 minutes +
30 minutes refrigeration
Total cooking time: 15 minutes
Makes 20

1½ cups plain flour
1 tablespoon custard powder
90 g unsalted butter
¼ cup caster sugar
1 egg yolk
2–3 tablespoons milk

Prune Filling
250 g cream cheese
⅓ cup caster sugar, extra
2 teaspoons grated lemon rind
1 cup chopped, pitted prunes

➤ BRUSH TWO 32 x 28 cm biscuit trays with melted butter or oil.

1 Place flour, custard powder, butter and sugar in food processor bowl. Using the pulse action, press button for 15 seconds or until mixture is fine and crumbly. Add egg yolk and milk; process 15 seconds or until mixture comes together. Turn onto a lightly floured surface; knead for 1 minute or until smooth. Roll out dough on baking paper to form a 30 x 28 cm rectangle.

2 To make Prune Filling: Using electric beaters, beat cream cheese, extra sugar and lemon rind in small mixing bowl until light and creamy. Using a flat-bladed knife, spread filling evenly over rolled-out dough. Top evenly with prunes.

3 Roll dough from one long side into the centre. Roll dough from the opposite side to meet in the centre. Refrigerate for 30 minutes or until firm. Heat oven to moderate 180°C. Using a sharp knife, cut into 1.5 cm slices. Place onto prepared trays, allowing room for spreading. Bake for 15 minutes or until lightly golden. Transfer biscuits to wire racks to cool.

COOK'S FILE

Storage time: Biscuits may be stored for three days in an airtight container or up to two months in the freezer.
Variation: Use dates or raisins instead of prunes. Orange rind can be used in place of lemon rind.
Hint: To save time, buy prunes which are already pitted.

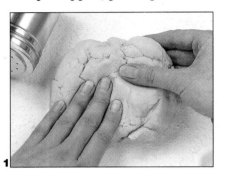

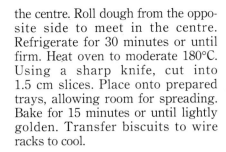

GOLDEN TRIANGLES

Preparation time: 20 minutes +
30 minutes refrigeration
Total cooking time: 10 minutes
Makes 40

125 g unsalted butter
2 tablespoons caster sugar
2 tablespoons golden syrup
½ cup currants
½ cup rolled oats
¾ cup plain flour
¼ cup rice flour

➤ BRUSH TWO 32 x 28 cm biscuit trays with melted butter or oil.

1 Using electric beaters, beat butter, sugar and golden syrup in a small mixing bowl until light and creamy. Transfer mixture to large mixing bowl; add currants and oats. Using a metal spoon, stir until combined. Add sifted flours; stir until combined.

2 Roll mixture into log shape, 20 cm long. Press log into triangular shape. Refrigerate for 30 minutes or until firm.

3 Heat oven to moderate 180°C. Cut log into 6 mm slices. Place slices onto prepared trays. Bake for 10 minutes or until lightly golden. Transfer to a wire rack to cool.

COOK'S FILE

Storage time: Biscuits may be stored up to four days in an airtight container or up to two months in the freezer.
Hint: Decorate with sifted icing sugar, if desired.
Variation: Replace golden syrup with honey, if preferred.
Use finely chopped raisins or sultanas instead of currants.

Prune and Cream Cheese Scrolls (top) and Golden Currant and Oat Triangles.

FRUITY MUESLI CAKES

Preparation time: 15 minutes
Total cooking time: 10 minutes
Makes about 30

1½ cups untoasted muesli
½ cup raw sugar
½ cup chopped glacé cherries
½ cup chopped dried
    apricots
½ cup roasted, unsalted
    peanuts
½ cup shredded coconut
½ cup plain flour
¼ cup sunflower seeds
125 g unsalted butter, melted
2 eggs, lightly beaten

➤ PREHEAT OVEN to moderate 180°C. Brush two 32 x 28 cm biscuit trays with melted butter or oil.

1 Place muesli, sugar, cherries, apricots, peanuts, coconut, flour and sunflower seeds in large mixing bowl; stir to combine.

2 Add butter. Using a metal spoon, stir until combined. Add eggs; mix well.

3 Drop tablespoons of mixture onto prepared trays. Bake for 10 minutes or until lightly golden. Transfer to wire racks to cool.

COOK'S FILE

Storage time: Store for up to two days in an airtight container or up to two months in the freezer.

Variation: These cakes are delicious drizzled with Lemon Glacé Icing or melted chocolate.

1

2

3

1

2

3

4

FLORENTINE TRIANGLES

Preparation time: 20 minutes
Total cooking time: 20 minutes
Makes 24

1¹/2 **cups slivered almonds**
2 **cups crushed cornflakes**
¹/2 **cup sultanas**
¹/2 **cup chopped glacé cherries**
¹/2 **cup chopped glacé pineapple**
¹/2 **cup chopped glacé apricots**
³/4 **cup condensed milk**
200 g **milk chocolate, chopped**
15 g **white vegetable shortening**

➤ PREHEAT OVEN to moderate 180°C. Brush a 30 x 25 x 2 cm Swiss roll tin with melted butter or oil. Cover base with paper, extending over two sides; grease paper.

1 Place almonds, cornflakes, sultanas, cherries, pineapple and apricots in a large mixing bowl. Using a metal spoon, stir until combined. Add condensed milk; stir until combined.

2 Press mixture into prepared tin. Bake for 15 minutes or until lightly golden. Stand 5 minutes before turning out onto wire rack to cool; remove paper.

3 Using a sharp knife, cut slice into 8 cm squares; cut each square diagonally in half.

4 Combine chocolate and shortening in small pan; stir over low heat until chocolate has melted. Remove from heat. Using a flat-bladed knife, spread half of each triangle with chocolate mixture; allow excess to run off. Place on wire rack to set.

COOK'S FILE

Storage time: Slice may be stored for up to two days in an airtight container.

Variation: Use dark or white chocolate instead of milk chocolate.

LEMON POPPYSEED MUSHROOMS

Preparation time: 20 minutes
Total cooking time: 10 minutes
Makes 24

60 g unsalted butter
60 g cream cheese
1/3 cup caster sugar
1 teaspoon finely grated
   lemon rind
1/4 cup poppyseeds
1/4 cup desiccated coconut
1 cup self-raising
   flour

Lemon Glacé Icing
1/2 cup pure icing sugar, sifted
1 tablespoon lemon juice

➤ PREHEAT OVEN to moderate 180°C. Brush two 32 x 28 cm biscuit trays with melted butter or oil.
1 Using electric beaters, beat butter, cream cheese, sugar and lemon rind in a small mixing bowl until light and creamy. Transfer to a medium mixing bowl. Add poppyseeds and coconut. Using a metal spoon, stir until combined. Add sifted flour; combine.
2 Roll mixture between two sheets of baking paper to 4 mm thickness.

Cut into mushrooms, using a floured, mushroom-shaped biscuit cutter. Place onto prepared trays. Bake for 10 minutes or until lightly golden. Transfer to wire racks to cool.
3 To make Lemon Glacé Icing: Combine icing sugar and lemon juice in a small bowl. Stand bowl over pan of simmering water, stirring until icing is smooth and glossy; remove from heat. Dip tops of biscuits into icing. Stand on wire rack until set.

C O O K ' S   F I L E

Storage time: Store up to three days in an airtight container or up to two months in freezer, without icing.

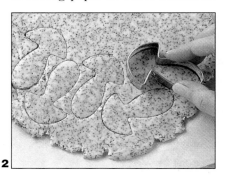

DATE AND LIME SLICE

Preparation time: 15 minutes
Total cooking time: 30 minutes
Makes 15

1 cup self-raising flour
1/2 cup caster sugar
1 cup desiccated coconut
2 teaspoons finely grated lime
   rind
1 cup chopped dates
1/2 cup chopped walnuts
180 g unsalted butter, melted
1 egg, lightly beaten
1 lime
1/2 cup caster sugar
1/4 cup water

Lime Icing
1 1/2 cups icing sugar, sifted
15 g unsalted butter,
   melted
1–2 tablespoons lime juice

➤ PREHEAT OVEN to moderate 180°C. Brush a 27 x 18 cm rectangular cake tin with melted butter or oil. Cover base with paper, extending over two sides; grease paper.
1 Place sifted flour, sugar, coconut, lime rind, dates and walnuts in a medium mixing bowl. Using a metal spoon, stir until combined.
2 Add butter; mix well. Add egg; stir until combined. Press into prepared tin. Bake for 20 minutes or until lightly golden. Stand 5 minutes

before turning out onto wire rack.
3 To make Lime Icing: Combine icing sugar in small mixing bowl with butter and lime juice. Spread evenly over slice; stand until set. Cut into squares. Cut lime rind into fine strips. Combine rind, sugar and water in small pan. Stir over low heat for 3 minutes or until sugar dissolves. Simmer, uncovered without stirring, for 5 minutes. Lift rind onto wire rack to drain. Use to decorate slice.

C O O K ' S   F I L E

Storage time: Slice may be stored up to three days in an airtight container or up to two months in freezer, without icing.

*Lemon Poppyseed Mushrooms (top) and
Date and Lime Slice.*

Sensational SAVOURIES

SUNFLOWER AND PARMESAN BISCUITS

Preparation time: 30 minutes
Total cooking time: 10–15 minutes
Makes 30

150 g unsalted butter
3/4 cup grated parmesan cheese
1/3 cup grated cheddar cheese
1 1/4 cups plain flour
2–3 teaspoons lemon pepper seasoning
1/4 cup sunflower seeds
1/4 cup grated parmesan cheese, extra

➤ PREHEAT OVEN to moderate 180°C. Line two oven trays with baking paper.

1 Using electric beaters, beat butter until light and creamy. Add parmesan and cheddar cheeses and beat until combined.

2 Using a metal spoon, fold in sifted flour and seasoning. Add sunflower seeds. Combine mixture with well-floured hand. Turn onto lightly floured surface and knead 2–3 minutes or until smooth.

3 Roll out dough between two sheets of baking paper to 5 mm thickness. Cut into squares, using a floured 4 cm-square biscuit cutter. Place on prepared trays, allowing room for spreading. Sprinkle the top of each biscuit with a little extra parmesan cheese. Bake for 10–15 minutes or until golden. Allow biscuits to cool on trays.

COOK'S FILE

Storage time: Biscuits may be stored in an airtight container in a cool dry place for up to two days.

Hints: Biscuits can also be cut in a variety of other shapes and sizes, for example rounds or stars.

Serve with drinks or as an accompaniment to soup or salad.

Variations: Use two to three teaspoons of French onion soup mix to replace the lemon pepper.

Add one tablespoon of freshly chopped herbs (chives, parsley, basil, thyme or rosemary), to mixture with the sunflower seeds.

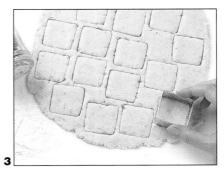

CHICKEN AND CORN BITES

Preparation time: 15 minutes
Total cooking time: 15 minutes
Makes 50

1 1/2 cup self-raising flour
1/2 cup (50 g) crushed
   corn-flavoured chips
2 teaspoons chicken stock
   powder

1/2 teaspoon chicken salt
60 g butter, chopped
2 eggs
chicken salt, extra

➤ PREHEAT OVEN to moderate 180°C. Line a 32 x 28 cm biscuit tray with baking paper.

1 Place flour, chips, powder and salt in food processor bowl; add butter. Using pulse button, press button for 15 seconds or until fine and crumbly.

2 Add eggs to bowl, process 5 sec-

onds or until mixture forms a soft dough. Turn dough onto lightly floured surface; knead 1 minute. Roll dough to 4 mm thickness. Cut into shapes using a plain or fluted biscuit cutter.

3 Place on prepared tray; sprinkle with chicken salt. Bake 15 minutes or until lightly browned. Cool on tray.

COOK'S FILE

Storage time: Store in airtight container for up to two days.

CHEESY CHILLI SESAME BALLS

Preparation time: 5 minutes
Total cooking time: 20 minutes
Makes 40 balls

1¼ cups plain flour
½ teaspoon chilli powder
125 g butter, chopped
40 g cream cheese, chopped
1 cup grated cheddar cheese
½ cup grated parmesan cheese
1 tablespoon chopped fresh
   coriander or parsley
⅔ cup sesame seeds

➤ PREHEAT OVEN to moderate 180°C. Line a 32 x 28 cm biscuit tray with baking paper.

1 Place flour and chilli into food processor bowl; add butter, cheeses and coriander.

2 Using the pulse action, press button for 15–20 seconds or until mixture almost forms a soft dough; do not overbeat. Turn mixture into a large mixing bowl; press together with fingers to form a soft dough.

3 Roll two level teaspoons of mixture into balls. Roll each ball in sesame seeds; arrange on prepared tray about 3 cm apart. Bake 20–25 minutes or until golden. Cool on trays.

COOK'S FILE

Storage time: Store up to two days in an airtight container.

1

2

3

HERBED CHEESE CRACKERS

Preparation time: 40 minutes
Total cooking time: 8 minutes each tray
Makes 20

Biscuit Pastry
1 cup plain flour
1/2 teaspoon baking powder
60 g butter
1 egg, lightly beaten
1 tablespoon iced water
1/2 cup grated cheddar
　　cheese
1 teaspoon chopped fresh
　　chives
1 teaspoon chopped fresh
　　parsley

Cheese Filling
80 g cream cheese
20 g butter
1 tablespoon chopped fresh
　　chives
1 tablespoon chopped
　　fresh parsley
1/4 teaspoon lemon pepper
3/4 cup grated cheddar cheese

➤ PREHEAT OVEN to moderately hot 210°C (190°C gas). Line two oven trays with baking paper.

1 To make Biscuit Pastry: Place flour and baking powder in food processor bowl; add chopped butter. Using the pulse action, press button for 30 seconds or until mixture is fine and crumbly.

2 Add egg, water and cheese to bowl and process 40 seconds or until mixture comes together. Turn out onto lightly floured surface, and knead herbs into pastry lightly, until smooth.

3 Roll pastry between sheets of baking paper to 3 mm thickness. Cut into rounds, using a 5 cm fluted cutter. Place rounds onto prepared trays. Re-roll remaining pastry and repeat cutting. Bake 8 minutes or until lightly browned. Transfer pastry rounds to wire rack to cool.

4 To make Cheese Filling: Using electric beaters, beat cream cheese and butter in small mixing bowl until light and creamy. Add herbs, pepper and cheese. Beat until smooth. Spread half a teaspoon of filling on the biscuits and sandwich together with the remaining biscuits.

COOK'S FILE

Storage time: Unfilled biscuits can be made two days ahead and stored in an airtight container. Cheese filling can be made a day ahead and stored, covered, in the refrigerator.

Variation: Use freshly chopped lemon thyme in place of parsley.
Hint: Pipe cheese mixture onto each biscuit without sandwiching together and serve with drinks as an hors d' oeuvre.

PIZZA SLICE

Preparation time: 15 minutes
Total cooking time: 35 minutes
Makes 20 pieces

375 g packet puff pastry
1/3 cup tomato paste
1 egg yolk
1 onion, grated
3 teaspoons dried oregano
  leaves
2 cups (250 g) grated
  mozzarella cheese
1 cup (100 g) finely
  chopped salami
1 green capsicum, finely
  chopped
1 tablespoon finely chopped
  black olives

➤ PREHEAT OVEN to moderately hot 210°C (190°C gas). Brush a shallow 30 x 25 x 2 cm Swiss roll tin with melted butter or oil.

1 Roll pastry between two sheets of plastic wrap, large enough to cover base of prepared tin. Prick pastry evenly with a fork. Bake 15 minutes, remove from oven.

2 Combine tomato paste, egg yolk, onion and two teaspoons oregano leaves in a small bowl. Spread the mixture evenly over pastry; sprinkle with half the grated cheese. Top with combined salami, capsicum and olives.

3 Sprinkle remaining cheese and oregano over slice. Bake 20 minutes or until crisp and golden. Transfer slice to wire rack to cool.

COOK'S FILE

Storage time: Pizza Slice is best eaten on the day it is made. It may be frozen as soon as it is cooled and reheated in a moderate 180°C oven for about 15 minutes before serving.

1

3

BACON AND MUSHROOM CREAM SLICE

Preparation time: 15 minutes
Total cooking time: 40 minutes
Makes 23 cm square (18 triangles)

1 egg yolk, lightly beaten
2 sheets ready-rolled
    shortcrust pastry
2 tablespoons oil
3 cups (375 g) finely chopped
    mushrooms
4 rashers bacon, finely
    chopped
4 spring onions, finely chopped
¼ cup finely chopped parsley

salt and pepper to taste
250 g cream cheese, softened
3 eggs, plus 1 egg white

➤ PREHEAT OVEN to moderately hot 210°C (190°C gas). Brush a shallow 23 cm square cake tin with melted butter or oil.

1 Brush yolk over one sheet of pastry. Place second sheet over first; press together gently. Trim pastry edges to fit tin. Prick pastry evenly with a fork. Bake 15 minutes; remove from oven.

2 Heat oil in heavy-based pan. Add mushrooms and stir over medium heat for 10 minutes or until mushrooms are well browned. Remove pan from heat. Stir in bacon, spring onions, and parsley. Season to taste; cool.

3 Using electric beaters, beat cheese and eggs in small mixing bowl on medium speed for 5 minutes. Add cooled mushroom mixture; stir to combine. Pour mixture onto partly cooked pastry base. Bake 25 minutes or until firm and lightly browned. Cool in tin. Cut into 18 triangles when cool.

COOK'S FILE

Storage time: Slice is best eaten on the day it is made.
Hint: This may be served as a savoury slice for morning tea, or cut into larger pieces and served for brunch with salad.

TOMATO AND GARLIC STICKS

Preparation time: 15 minutes
Total cooking time: 15–20 minutes
Makes 48

100 g sun-dried tomatoes
    in olive oil
1 clove garlic, crushed
1 tablespoon chopped black
    olives
1 teaspoon capers
¼ teaspoon dried oregano
black pepper to taste
2 sheets puff pastry

1 egg, lightly beaten
1 tablespoon poppyseeds

➤ PREHEAT OVEN to moderately hot 210°C (190°C gas). Line a 32 x 28 cm biscuit tray with baking paper.

1 Drain tomatoes, reserving two teaspoons of oil. Place in food processor bowl with garlic, olives, capers, oregano and pepper. Using pulse action, press button 2 minutes or until smooth.

2 Spread tomato mixture on one sheet of pastry. Top with remaining pastry sheet; press sheet down well to join. Cut into three strips. Cut

each strip into 16 smaller strips.
3 Brush pastry with egg. Sprinkle with poppyseeds and bake for 15–20 minutes, or until puffed and golden. Serve hot or cold.

COOK'S FILE

Storage time: Store up to two days in an airtight container. Sticks may be frozen, uncooked, up to two months.
Variation: Use green olives in place of black olives.
Hint: Sun-dried tomatoes are available either loose or in oil. Loose tomatoes may be rehydrated in hot water until plump. Drain and use as required.

Bacon and Mushroom Cream Slice (top) and Tomato and Garlic Sticks.

FRENCH ONION CRACKERS

Preparation time: 20 minutes
Total cooking time: 20 minutes
Makes about 50

2 cups plain flour
1/4 cup cornflour
2 tablespoons French onion
   soup mix
2 teaspoons dried chives
125 g unsalted butter
1/2 cup sour cream

➤ PREHEAT OVEN to moderate 180°C. Line two 32 x 28 cm biscuit trays with baking paper.

1 Place flours, soup mix, chives and butter in food processor bowl. Using pulse action, press button for 30 seconds or until mixture is fine and crumbly.

2 Add sour cream and process further 30 seconds until mixture forms a dough. Turn out onto a lightly floured surface; knead 30 seconds or until smooth.

3 Trying to keep it to a rectangle shape, roll out dough to 5 mm thick.

Using a knife or pastry cutter, cut dough into 4 cm squares. Place on prepared tray and prick with a fork. Bake for 20 minutes or until just golden. Transfer crackers to a wire rack to cool.

COOK'S FILE

Storage time: Crackers may be stored for up to two days in an airtight container.
Variation: Use one tablespoon fresh chopped chives to replace the dried.
Hint: Serve crackers with soup, or with a pâté and drinks.

1

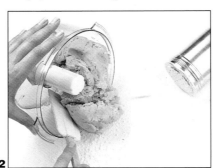

2

3

INDEX

ICINGS, TOPPINGS AND FILLINGS

SAVOURY

SLICES

USEFUL INFORMATION

All our recipes are thoroughly tested in the *Family Circle* Test Kitchen. Standard metric measuring cups and spoons approved by Standards Australia are used in the development of our recipes. All cup and spoon measurements are level. We have used 60 g eggs in all recipes. Can sizes vary from manufacturer to manufacturer and between countries; use the can size closest to the one suggested in the recipe.

Australian Metric Cup and Spoon Measures

For dry ingredients the standard set of metric measuring cups consists of 1 cup, ½ cup, ⅓ cup and ¼ cup sizes.

For measuring liquids, a transparent, graduated measure is available in either a 250 mL cup or a 1 litre jug.

The basic set of metric spoons, used to measure both dry and liquid ingredients, is made up of 1 tablespoon, 1 teaspoon, ½ teaspoon and ¼ teaspoon.

Note: Australian tablespoon equals 20 mL. British, US and NZ tablespoons equal 15 mL for use in liquid measuring. The teaspoon has a 5 mL capacity and is the same for Australian, British and American markets.

Ingredients in Grams (Aust. Cups)

	1 cup	1¼ cups	1½ cups	1¾ cups	2 cups
Breadcrumbs					
fine, fresh	60	75	90	105	120
dried	90	115	135	155	180
Cocoa Powder					
	85	105	125	150	170
Coconut					
desiccated	75	95	115	130	150
Flour					
	150	190	225	265	300
Sugar					
soft brown	165	205	245	285	330
caster	220	275	330	385	440
granulated	220	275	330	385	440
demerara	205	255	310	360	410
icing	160	200	240	280	320
raw	215	270	325	380	430

Oven Temperatures

Electric	C	F
Very slow	120	250
Slow	150	300
Mod slow	160	325
Moderate	180	350
Mod hot	210	425
Hot	240	475
Very hot	260	525

Gas	C	F
Very slow	120	250
Slow	150	300
Mod slow	160	325
Moderate	180	350
Mod hot	190	375
Hot	200	400
Very hot	230	450

British and American Cup and Spoon Conversion

Australian	*British/American*
1 tablespoon	3 teaspoons
2 tablespoons	¼ cup
¼ cup	⅓ cup
⅓ cup	½ cup
½ cup	⅔ cup
⅔ cup	¾ cup
¾ cup	1 cup
1 cup	1¼ cups

Glossary

Australian	*British/American*	*Australian*	*British/American*
Unsalted butter	Unsalted butter/sweet butter	Glacé fruit	Glacé fruit/candied fruit
125 g butter	125 g butter/1 stick of butter	Icing sugar	Icing sugar/superfine sugar
Bicarbonate of soda	Bicarbonate of soda/ baking soda	Plain flour	Plain flour/all-purpose flour
Caster sugar	Castor sugar/superfine sugar	Self-raising	Self-raising/self-rising flour
Cornflour	Cornflour/cornstarch	Sultanas	Golden raisins/seedless white raisins
Essence	Essence/extract		

4462
This edition published in 1998 by Colour Library Direct, a division of Quadrillion Publishing Ltd, Godalming, Surrey, GU7 1XW
Originally published in Australia by Murdoch Books, a division of Murdoch Magazines Pty Ltd, 213 Miller Street, North Sydney NSW 2060
© 1992 & 1993 photography and illustrations: Murdoch Books. All rights reserved. No part of this publication may be reproduced, stored in any retrieval system or transmitted in any form or by any means, electronic, mechanical, photocopying, recording or otherwise without the prior written permission of the publisher and copyright holder.
Murdoch Books is a registered trademark of Murdoch Magazines Pty Ltd.
ISBN 1-85833-471-3
Printed and bound in the United Arab Emirates

Murdoch Books Food Editor: Kerrie Ray
Family Circle Food Editor: Jo Anne Calabria
Home Economists: Tracy Rutherford, Voula Mantzouridis, Melanie McDermott, Kerrie Ray, Kerrie Carr
Photography: Jon Bader
Step-by-step Photography: Reg Morrison
Food Stylist: Carolyn Fienberg, Mary Harris
Food Stylist's Assistants: Jo Forrest, Rebecca Clancy, Tracey Port
Publisher: Anne Wilson
Publishing Manager: Mark Newman
Managing Editors: Lynn Humphries and Susan Tomnay
Art Director: Lena Lowe
Production Manager: Catie Ziller

1 cm 2 cm 3 cm 4 cm 5 cm 6 cm 7 cm 8 cm 9 cm 10 cm 11 cm 12 cm 13 cm 14 cm 15 cm 16 cm 17 cm 18 cm 19 cm 20 cm 21 cm 22 cm 23 cm 24 cm 25 cm